Handbook of Greek Pottery

HANDBOOK
OF
GREEK POTTERY

A Guide for Amateurs

ROBERT S. FOLSOM

Illustrated by the author

FABER AND FABER LIMITED
24 Russell Square
London

First published in mcmlxvii
by Faber and Faber Limited
24 Russell Square London W.C.1
Printed in Great Britain by
Ebenezer Baylis and Son Limited
The Trinity Press Worcester and London

Foreword and Acknowledgments

Every visitor to Greece is intrigued by the fragments of ancient pottery (potsherds) that litter the ancient sites. Shortly after my arrival in Greece in October 1958, I too became intrigued by ancient Greek pottery. Seeing examples in museums and private collections and finding potsherds almost everywhere I went stimulated my interest. I soon found that I had passed beyond the initial stage of merely seeing the pots and the bits and pieces, and that I now wanted to know their age and origin. Baulked by my own lack of knowledge, I turned first to archaeologist friends for identification of my sherds. This soon proved too cumbersome for me and burdensome to them. Next I sought a solution in bookshops. I amassed in a short time a fine (and expensive) shelf of books on Greek pottery written by archaeologists, ceramics experts and artists – each presented from the point of view of the author, but none providing in compact and coherent form the data needed for quick and relatively accurate identification. I then began to compile a notebook using my books, and other people's books too, and my archaeologist friends' and my own experience. The present handbook for amateurs by an amateur is the result.

I have sought to select those salient features of each type, style and technique which provide easy identification. Thus for the period under reference, 1050 B.C. to 146 B.C., I have used the following outline:

Background (the colour and texture of the bulk of the pot – on which the decoration is painted).

Decoration (a general description of the type of decoration employed – geometric designs, animal figures, human figures, historical scenes, scenes from daily life, etc.).

Repertory of Designs (a listing of the types of abstract, floral, animal, human and fantastic figures making up the total decoration).

Shapes of Pots (whether large or small, amphorae, hydriai, etc.).

Clay (colour, coarseness and other identifying characteristics).

It is my hope that with such data available, the owners of this handbook may enjoy at least some success in determining the age and origin of ancient Greek pots and sherds.

Inevitably, I was led into two other areas: (1) identification of the various shapes, and (2) description of the latest theories and discoveries in the fields of pot-making and the decoration of ancient Greek pottery.

Initially, I used Arthur Lane's *Greek Pottery* (Faber and Faber, London, 1948 (new edition 1963)). This I supplemented with R. M. Cook's *Greek Painted Pottery* (Methuen, London, 1960); and finally I employed *A History of Greek Vase Painting* by P. E. Arias and M. Hirmer (Thames and Hudson, London, 1962) to fill out my remaining gaps – for both the basic outlines and detailed information on the various types, styles and techniques.

I used these three works and *Shapes and Names of Athenian Vases* by G. M. A. Richter and M. J. Milne (Metropolitan Museum of Art, New York, 1935) in making the sketches and silhouettes of the shapes of Greek pottery.

Acknowledgment for material contained in the section called 'Techniques and Mediums Used' must be given to various authors. For the steps in making pots I have drawn on descriptions contained in R. M. Cook's *Greek Painted Pottery* and Arthur Lane's *Greek Pottery*, and, in particular, on an article by Joseph V. Noble entitled 'The Technique of Attic Vase-Painting' published in the *American Journal of Archeology* (Archeological Institute of America, Princeton, N.J., Vol. 64, No. 4). For the data presented on the art of creating the red, black and fine sheen of pots, credit must be given to G. M. A. Richter for her work in solving the mystery of 'painting' on Greek pottery (*The Craft of Athenian Pottery*, New Haven, 1923); to Dr. Theodor Schumann for his reproduction of the ancient black glaze in 1942 ('Oberflachen-verzierung in der antiken Topferkunst. Terra Sigillata und Griechische Schwarzrotmalerei', published in *Berichte der deutschen keramischen Gesellschaft*, 23, 1942, pp. 408–426); to Marie Farnsworth and Harriet Wisely for their reproduction of the ancient red glaze ('Fifth Century Intentional Red Glaze', published in the *American Journal of Archeology*, Vol. 62, No. 2, 1958); and to Joseph V. Noble for his study of the use of accessory colours – the means by which the black glaze and other colours were applied – for his reproduction of the celebrated Attic relief line, and for his analyses of Greek clays ('The Technique of Attic Vase-Painting' cited above). Cook and Lane provide summaries of information on decoration and firing which I have also used.

Individuals to whom I owe a debt of gratitude include: Dr. Photios Petsas of the Greek Archaeological Service for encouragement and suggestions; Professor Eugene Vanderpool and Michael Katzev of the American School of Classical Studies in Athens for their co-operation, criticisms, and time; Charles H. Morgan of the Department of Fine Arts, Amherst College, for his helpful hints and suggested additions; former Dean at Anatolia College, William Sanford, and his wife Ariadne for their encouragement over the publication of my manuscript; friends who have loaned me books, notably Terence and

Helen Woods-Smith; my secretary, Bernice Kauerz, for her endless patience; and finally my wife, for not leaving me when for so many months I preferred my pots to hers.

Thessaloniki, Greece
February 1964

Contents

PART 4:

SHAPES AND USES OF GREEK POTTERY

APPENDIX 1: PAINTING AND DESIGN
(ADDITIONAL INFORMATION)

APPENDIX 2: SHAPES AND USES OF GREEK POTTERY (DETAILED ACCOUNT)

List of Plates

with acknowledgments and references

* The numbers in brackets are those used to identify the pottery.

Introduction

This handbook has been compiled as a quick, easy guide for the amateur of Greek pottery in the hope that, within reasonable limits, it will enable him to identify and better appreciate the major types of pottery seen in museums and at excavation sites.

Though mention is made of Cretan and Helladic pottery of the period prior to 1050 B.C. and of Hellenistic pottery subsequent to 323 B.C., emphasis is placed on the Greek pottery produced between these dates, an age in which it flourished as a major art, fulfilling to a unique degree three functions – utility, beauty of form and beauty of decoration. Later, form was sacrificed to utility, while as an art form the pot was replaced by other media.

Similarly, this handbook is restricted to the pottery of major centres of production and to the more important types. More than fifty centres in mainland Greece, the Greek areas of Asia Minor, Italy, and Sicily, and the Islands produced known wares; and in every Greek settlement there must have been some local production. Over more than eight hundred years local artisans developed new schools and styles that brought their cities to prominence at least briefly before other new schools replaced them in public favour. To trace all these developments in one book would be tedious and confusing.

In brief, what is presented here is a sketch of the main lines of development with only a few excursions to mention the more interesting minor styles.

The story begins about 1050 B.C. with the pottery of the *Proto-Geometric* period, which represents a clear break from the preceding *Mycenaean* with its curving lines and stylized floral decoration, towards formal geometric designs. Pottery of the *Geometric* period which followed and was produced from 900 to 700 B.C., is characterized by monotone dark browns and black against a lighter background almost completely covered by abstract geometric designs, with human and animal forms rarely being represented and then only in angular silhouette. Attica was the major centre of production for geometric pottery. Under an *orientalizing* influence, which brought in the freer use of curves, new ornaments, and flora and fauna, this style gradually gave way in the *Archaic* period (700 to 480 B.C.) first to animal and later to human forms of design. The figures were painted in black against a lighter background. Corinth, with its orientalized *animal style* in which poses were formal (e.g. animals or birds in rows, or in confronting pairs, or less formally in threes) and overlapping of figures was rare, dominated until about 550 B.C. At this point a new Attic style with *human* forms, informality of pose and overlapping of figures replaced 'Corinthian'. This *Black Figure* technique, painted in shiny black against a bright orange-red background (or more rarely on a white ground) with incised detail and profile figures, is austere but striking. The favourite subjects for depiction were the gods and heroes of the Greek myths in action, often in battle scenes. With the development of the *Red Figure* technique in Athens after about 530 B.C., the background was painted black, the figures were left in red-orange silhouette, and details were filled in with painted lines instead of incisions. Thus a more natural and less stiff and less austere type of painting became possible. The subject-matter turned from mythology to scenes from daily life, with emphasis being laid on anatomy and mood instead of action. During the Late Archaic period, Attic Black Figure and Red Figure co-existed and dominated Greek pottery. In the Classical period (480–323 B.C.) Red Figure supplanted Black Figure, the three-quarters and full-face view replaced the profile view; the profile eye replaced the Archaic full eye; and the designs became more florid. Lack of depth in depiction of scenes could no longer be ignored and artists turned from vase-painting to other media. The decline of Greek painted pottery had begun.

This, in summary, is the story of Greek painted pottery. The sequence is: Proto-Geometric – Geometric – Orientalizing Influence – Archaic Animal Style (Corinth) – Attic Black Figure and Red Figure – Classical Athenian. To restrict the story, however, to this bare outline would do injustice to other areas and other schools. The more important of these clearly justify some mention. Among these are the Cycladic, the East Greek and the Laconian styles, at the very least. Whether other areas of production, other schools and styles should be mentioned is, of course, open to debate. Some of these have been included in the various appendices. Those interested in a book with more detail with photographic plates but restricted to about the same scope as this handbook are referred to Arthur Lane's *Greek Pottery*. Those desiring to trace Greek pottery in greater detail and discover about other centres, additional types and styles are referred to R. M. Cook's *Greek Painted Pottery*, which also contains a bibliography for additional detailed specialization. For those who do not worry about 'excess baggage', *A History of Greek Vase Painting* by P. E. Arias and M. Hirmer is a beautiful and useful addition.

Identification of ancient Greek pottery by the complete neophyte, whether as whole pots or as potsherds, is difficult. The purpose of this handbook is to ease this task.

Parts 1 to 4 provide the beginner with a general chronology, information about the techniques and mediums used in the production of ancient Greek pottery, and sufficient data on painting, design, uses and shapes to enable him to make at least tentative identifications.

Those who wish to delve deeper into the subject will find that the various appendices elaborate on the somewhat broad treatment provided in the main text.

The book is thus in two depths, and should be used according to the interests of the reader.

Part 1
CHRONOLOGY

Chronological Summary

A. POTTERY: CHARACTERISTICS AND DEVELOPMENTS

CRETAN 2800–1100 B.C.
> EARLY MINOAN
> 2800–2000 B.C.
> MIDDLE MINOAN
> 2000–1550 B.C.
> LATE MINOAN
> 1550–1100 B.C.

HELLADIC 2800–1100 B.C.
Cretan pottery with its flowing lines and decoration of the whole pot appears to have influenced Helladic pottery. Mycenaean pottery of the late Helladic period was characterized by flowing lines and stripes embracing the whole pot.
> EARLY HELLADIC
> 2800–1900 B.C.
> MIDDLE HELLADIC
> 1900–1550 B.C.
> LATE HELLADIC
> 1550–1100 B.C.
>> MYCENAEAN I
>> 1550–1500 B.C.
>> MYCENAEAN II
>> 1500–1425 B.C.
>> MYCENAEAN III
>> 1425–1100 B.C.

'SUB-MYCENAEAN' 1100–1050 B.C.
'Sub-Mycenaean' pottery continued the Mycenaean tradition, but designs were lifeless, with ornamentation usually consisting of one broad band around the pot and three narrow bands above and below.

PROTO-GEOMETRIC 1050–900 B.C.
Characterized by compass-drawn circles and semi-circles, lozenges, chequers, triangles and swastikas, drawn solid, cross-hatched or dotted. Occasional silhouette horses (no other animals or humans).

GEOMETRIC 900–700 B.C.
The hatched meander is characteristic. Other geometric designs were hatched or cross-hatched. Concentric circles and semi-circles

disappeared. Humans and animals appeared in silhouette (thin, spiked, triangular-chested with match-stick limbs).

755–700 Period of great funerary amphorae.

725–700 Period of plastic forms on pottery.

ARCHAIC 700–480 B.C.

Influences from the East brought flowing lines, plant forms and new animals.

710–610 Period when perforated handles were common.

c. 650 One of the earliest potter's signatures (Aristonothos).

c. 630 Possibly the first painter's signature (Istrokles?).

600–500 Period when panel amphorae were common.

c. 550 'Kalos' inscriptions appear and persist into the 5th century.

CORINTHIAN (dominant)

700–550

725–625 *Proto-Corinthian*

Characterized by introduction of flowing lines, plants and animals along with older geometric designs. Parallel lines and stalked dot rosettes are particularly characteristic, as is the small thin-walled skyphos or kotyle shape.

c. 700 Introduction of *incision.*

c. 700 Introduction of Hittite lion, sphinx, and other strange animals from the East.

625–550 *Corinthian Animal Style*

Predominance of animals (full-face panther, Assyrian lion and a great variety of weird animals, such as griffins, gorgons, etc.). The stalked dot rosette degenerated to an incised blob.

LACONIAN

700–500

700–630 *Laconian I* (Reserving Period)

Characterized by rows of squares between two rows of dots, broad painted areas and bands of purple.

630–590 *Laconian II* (Early Black Figure)

Birds are most characteristic, along with pomegranates; squares between two rows of dots became more widely spaced. Incision was used only for outlines of figures.

590–525 *Laconian III and IV* (Developed Black Figure)

Animals and humans in scenes from mythology are characteristic.

CYCLADIC

700–650

(Includes Theran, Wheel Group, Linear Island Group, 'AD Group', 'Heraldic Group', Protome Group and Melian)

Though groups vary, they are characterized by wiry, boneless animals with white faces and solid, dotted or chequered bodies. Painting is done with broad strokes. No incision.

EAST GREEK

650–500

The 'wild goat' is the most characteristic design along with other animals and birds. Filling designs include hooked swastikas, pendant triangles, concentric semi-circles, cables, etc., all drawn free-hand and in careless reserved style.

ATTIC

710–480

710–610   *Proto-Attic*

Along with older geometric designs, animals and humans appeared in black silhouette with reserved faces. Figures are poorly planned and ill-proportioned. Other designs include solid rays, hooked spirals, spotted leaves, cables, etc. The whole surface of the pot was regarded as a single field for decoration. Scenes began to portray mythological events.

Mid 7th century   Appearance of white paint on Attic pottery.

Third quarter of 7th century   Appearance of red paint on Attic pottery.

610–450*   *Black Figure Technique*

Gods, humans and mythological figures appeared, first in narrative style, later in scenes depicting mood, and, finally, in scenes of everyday life. Humans were shown with frontal upper bodies and profile lower bodies. Faces were usually in profile, however, with a frontal eye. Incision was used for details. Scenes were concentrated in panels and bands. Titles appeared to identify the characters shown.

7th century   First appearance of frontal face (rare, though).

Early 6th century   First appearance of Dionysus and satyrs.

c. 575   First signature of an Attic artist (Sophilos).

c. 570   It became conventional to paint men in black and women in white.

c. 566–560   First Panathenaic amphorae given as prizes at the athletic games in honour of Athena. These continued to be produced in the Black Figure technique throughout the 3rd century B.C. Some time between 359 and 348 B.C. the position of

* Though the Archaic period technically ends with the year 480 B.C., production of painted pottery by the Black Figure technique continued into the Classical period with one special type, the Panathenaic amphora, continuing into the Hellenistic period.

Athena on the amphorae was changed from facing left; thereafter she faced to the right.

c. 550   Attic pottery obtained dominance over all other Greek pottery.

c. 520   With changes in style of clothing, the soft, short-sleeved chiton replaced the heavy, sleeveless peplos and more attention was given to drapery and folds.

530–480   *Archaic Red Figure Technique*

Mythological scenes were almost completely replaced by scenes from everyday life. Poses became more natural with the torso shown in profile, full, or three-quarters view. The three-quarter face appeared and the profile eye began to replace the Archaic frontal eye in profile faces. Hair outline was reserved instead of incised. Ornamentation, except in the human figures featured in the main panels, tended to become scarce.

End of 6th century   White ground pottery for use with both Black and Red Figure techniques was introduced.

CLASSICAL 480–323 B.C.

Scenes were drawn primarily from life and were cheerful. Details were painted, not incised. The painting became more important than the pot. Furniture and, later, figures were painted in perspective. Great attention was given to contours and to shape and fall of dress. Scenes gradually became more crowded and fussy. A pair or trio of stereotyped youths became characteristic on the back of pots.

HELLENISTIC 323–146 B.C.

By the beginning of the Hellenistic period, painted pottery as an art form was dying; by the end of the period, it was dead. Hellenistic pottery is characterized by plastic decoration, relief and impression. The painting was simple and clearly painted on the pot – not an organic part of it. Wreaths, vines and festoons of ivy became common in styles that lacked both skill and imagination.

B. POTTERY: DATES FOR CERTAIN SHAPES

B.C.

1000–900 Globular pyxis	900–323 Kantharos
1000–450 Kyathos	850–650 Bell-mouthed oinochoe
1000–323 Skyphos	800–700 Flat pyxis
900–800 Pointed pyxis	800–700 Straight-sided pyxis
900–350 Neck amphora	800–600 'Standard' oinochoe

B.C.

725–625	Tall convex Corinthian pyxis
725–323	Corinthian aryballos
700–600	High convex pyxis
700–323	Alabastron
700–323	Askos
650–600	Attic kotyle krater
650–500	Wild Goat kotyle krater
650–200	Broad-bottomed oino-choe
625–425	Column krater
620–550	Chiot chalice
610–323	One-piece amphora
600–550	One-piece lekythos
600–500	Neck hydria
600–500	Attic tripod pyxis
600–323	Volute krater
585–570	Comast cup
575–550	Siana cup
565–535	Lip cup (Type I)
560–510	Droop cup
560–2nd C.	Panathenaic amphora

B.C.

550–520	Band cup
550–520	Attic aryballos
550–500	Type A (or Type II) Eye cup
550–323	Lekythos with angular shoulder
550–323	Calyx krater
525–323	Loutrophoros
520–450	Type B (or Type III) cup
520–450	Attic oinochoe
520–323	Low concave pyxis
500–400	One-piece hydria
500–323	Classical shape of lekythos
490–460	Type C lip cup
480–323	Classical cup
450–323	Squat lekythos
400–323	Bell krater
400–300	Cylindrical pyxis
323–200	Megarian bowl

C. POTTERS AND PAINTERS

Before the Archaic period of Greek pottery, conformity in production of pots, and especially in decoration, was the rule, and this inhibits the identification of either potters or painters. But with the introduction of new techniques individualism became the rule. Both potters and painters began to develop distinctive characteristics. Archaeologists have thus been able to give names to potters according to their style or the location of their workshops. By the middle of the 7th century B.C., however, identification becomes precise as potters with sufficient pride in their work began to sign their products with the phrase: '—— *m'epoiesen*' (μ'ἐποίησεν) ('—— made me'). It is believed that this phrase often meant the pot was both made and decorated by the potter named–for example, that Aristonothos, in signing a pot *Aristonothos m'epoiesen* about 650 B.C., was signing as both potter and painter. *M'epoiesen* signatures of Kallikleas, Pyrrhos and Nikesermos are also regarded as probably indicating both potter and painter. The phrase '—— *m'egrapsen*'

(μ'ἔγραψεν) ('—— painted me'), clearly distinguishing potter from
painter, appeared a little later chronologically. Istrokles may have
actually signed *m'egrapsen* about 630 B.C., but the evidence is in-
conclusive. The first certain *m'egrapsen* signature is on a Naxian fragment dated to the last quarter of the 7th century, but unfortunately
though the phrase *m'egrapsen* is clearly on the fragment, the artist's
name is lost. Next in time are the clearly recognizable *m'egrapsen*
signatures of Sophilos (590–570) and Kleitias (570–550).

Besides painters whose names are known from their signatures, many
others have been identified and given names by archaeologists. Such
names are based on:

A.* The names of the potters with whom they usually worked (e.g.
the Amasis Painter worked with the potter Amasis who signed his pots).

B. The name of a particular or favourite subject (such as the Gorgon
Painter or the Pan Painter).

C. The style of the painter (the C or Corinthian Painter).

D. The location of the collection which once contained or now contains the painter's most famous or first identified work (the Berlin and
Heidelberg Painters).

E. The place where the first instance–or most–of the artist's work
was found (the Naucratis, Eleusis and Eretria Painters).

F. The name of a former owner (the Barclay Painter).

G. The commonest or first identified 'love name' shown on pots of
the painter (the Kleophon Painter).

H. The favourite type of pot decorated by the artist (the Dinos
Painter).

Some of the more important potters and painters are given in the
following list:

LIST OF POTTERS AND PAINTERS

POTTERS (*m'epoiesen*)	PAINTERS (*m'egrapsen*)	APPROXIMATE DATE
I. *Orientalizing Style:*		
—	[E.] The Analatos Painter	First quarter of 7th century
Pyrrhos	Pyrrhos (?)	Early 7th century
—	[B.] The Menelaus Painter	Second quarter of 7th century
—.	[B.] The Ram Jug Painter	660–650
Aristonothos	Aristonothos (?)	Mid 7th century
Kallikleas	Kallikleas (?)	Mid 7th century
—	[D.] The MacMillan Painter	645–635

* These letters A–H are shown in the list of potters and painters below to aid in
identification of the origin of painters' names.

POTTERS (*m'epoiesen*)	PAINTERS (*m'egrapsen*)	APPROXIMATE DATE
Istrokles	Istrokles (?)	Third quarter of 7th century
—	Missing name on a Naxian fragment	Fourth quarter of 7th century
—	[B.] The Nettos (or Nessos) Painter	Fourth quarter of 7th century
Missing name from Selinus	—	Late 7th century
Nikesermos	Nikesermos (?)	End of 7th century

II. *Non-Attic Black Figure Styles:*

—	*Timonidas* (1)	580–570
—	[B.] The Hephaestos Painter (2)	590–550
—	[B.] The Arkesilas Painter (2)	565–560
—	[B.] The Naucratis Painter (2)	570–560
—	[B.] The Hunt Painter (2)	Mid 6th century
—	[C.] The Inscription Painter (3)	550–530
—	[B.] The Phineus Painter (3)	550–530
—	[H.] An unknown artist (4)	530–510

III. *Archaic Attic Black Figure Technique:*

—	[B.] The Gorgon Painter	First half of 6th century
—	*Sophilos* (5)	590–570
Cheiron	[C.] The Corinthian (or C) Painter (6)	575–550
—	[D.] The Heidelberg Painter (7)	575–550
Ergotimos	*Kleitias* (or Klitias or Kletias)	570–550
Tleson (8)	[A.] The Tleson Painter (8)	565–530
Phrynos (8)	[A.] The Phrynos Painter (8)	565–530
Kolchos, Amasis and Nikosthenes }	*Lydos*	560–540
Amasis	[A.] The Amasis Painter	560–520
Exekias	*Exekias*	550–520
Lysippides	[A.] The Lysippides Painter	530–500

IV. *Painters in both Red Figure and Black Figure Techniques – Originators of the Red Figure Technique:*

Andokides	[A.] The Andokides Painter	Last third of 6th century

Hilinos,   ⎞
    Andokides   ⎟   *Psiax* (9)   530–510

V. *Archaic Attic Red Figure Technique:*

Pamphaios,   ⎞
    Chelis,   ⎟
    Kachrylion, ⎟   *Oltos*   525–500
    Euxitheos   ⎟
    and   ⎟
    Tleson (?): ⎠

Hischylos,   ⎞
    Python,   ⎟
    Nikosthenes, ⎟
    Pamphaios,   ⎟   *Epiktetos*   520–500
    Andokides,   ⎟
    and   ⎟
    Pistoxenos: ⎠

Kachrylion and   ⎞
    Euxitheos: ⎠   *Euphronios* (10)   515–500

—   *Euthymides*   520/15–500
Phintias   *Phintias* (*Phintis,*
                           Phitias or Philtias)
Kleophrades   [A.] The Kleophrades Painter   500–480
Phintias   [D.] The Berlin Painter (11)   Late 6th to 570
Euphronios   *Onesimos* (12)   500–475
Brygos   [A.] The Brygos Painter   500–480
Hieron   *Makron*   495–480

Douris,   ⎞
    Python,   ⎟
    Kleophrades, ⎟   *Douris* (or *Doris*)   500–470
    Kalliades,   ⎟
    Euphronios: ⎠

VI. *Classical Attic Red Figure Technique:*

—   [B.] The Pan Painter   480–450
—   [B.] The Penthesileia Painter   465–450
Pistoxenos,   ⎞
    Megakles,   ⎟   [A.] The Pistoxenos Painter   475–450
    Euphronios: ⎠
—   [B.] The Niobid Painter   465–450
—   [D.] The Villa Giulia Painter   475–450
—   [B.] The Achilles Painter   460–430
—   [D.] The Mannheim Painter   Third quarter of
                                                           5th century

—	*Polygnotos*	445–430
—	[E.] The Eretria Painter	430–420

VII. *Late Fifth Century Attic Style:*

—	[G.] The Kleophon Painter	435–420
—	[H.] The Dinos Painter (13)	425–400
Meidias	[A.] The Medias Painter	Late 5th to early 4th century
—	[B.] The Talos Painter	Late 5th to early 4th century
—	[B.] The Pronomos Painter	Late 5th to early 4th century
—	[E.] The Suessula Painter	Late 5th to early 4th century

VIII. *Fourth Century Attic Painters:*

—	[D.] The Painter of the New York Centauromachy	400–360
—	[D.] The Jena Painter	400–360
—	[B.] The Meleager Painter	400–375
—	[B.] The Marsyas Painter	375–350

IX. *Etruscan, Apulian, Paestan and Lucanian Painters:*

—	[B.] The Aurora Painter (14)	Second quarter of 4th century
—	[B.] The Sisyphus Painter (15)	Last third of 4th century
—	[B.] The Darius Painter (15)	Last third of 4th century
—	[D.] The Tarporley Painter (15)	Last third of 4th century
—	*Asteas* (16)	Mid 4th century
—	*Python* (16)	Mid 4th century
—	[E.] The Pisticci Painter (17)	Last third of 4th century
—	[B.] The Karneia Painter (17)	Last third of 4th century

1. Names in italics are those of painters who actually signed *m'egrapse*. Timonidas is the only Corinthian painter whose name is known.
2. Laconian painters.
3. Painters who created the Chalcidian style which is represented by some 300 pots, all dated to the period 550–510 B.C.
4. The painter of Phocaea in Ionia who either exported some 30 'Caeretan' style hydriai to Caere in Italy, or migrated there and set up his workshop.
5. The signature of Sophilos is the earliest certain signature of an artist on an Attic vase.

6. The chief artist of the Siana cups.
7. Also a painter of Siana cups.
8. Potters and painters of Little Master cups. These cups bear some 30 different signatures, practically all potters' signatures.
9. Formerly known as the Menon Painter.
10. Euphronios was also a potter and worked in this capacity until about 460 B.C.
11. An artist previously known as the Vienna Painter has been shown to be identical with the Berlin Painter.
12. Also called the Panaitios Painter (from the *Kalos* (or love name) Panaitios).
13. Formerly called the Atalante Painter.
14. Etruscan painter.
15. Apulian Painters.
16. Paestan Painters.
17. Lucanian Painters.

Chronological Diagram: 1000–323 B.C.

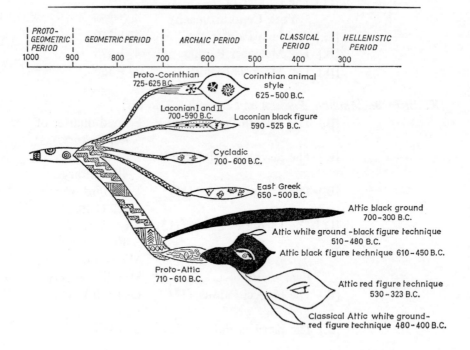

Part 2

TECHNIQUES AND MEDIUMS USED

Techniques and Mediums Used

BACKGROUND

Methods of production of the very fine shiny red and black colours employed by Greek potters* were a complete mystery for centuries. Until recently the sheen was described as a varnish or a glaze and the brilliant reds and blacks as paints. In fact, the sheen is neither a varnish nor a silicate or lead glaze, and the colours were not produced by application of colour pigments. Only in the years since World War II have techniques been developed which appear to duplicate the Attic product.

It has now been established that the 'paints' were dilute solutions of the same clay as that used in making the pot–solutions of such extremely fine clay particles as to constitute colloidal suspensions. To produce these solutions, two additional agents may have been employed. Humin (present, for example, in urine) may have been added to prevent coagulation. Potash almost certainly was added, not only to prevent coagulation, but also to make the suspension thinner and more fluid.

To understand how the ancient potters achieved their beautiful blacks, reds and orange-reds using a 'paint' made from the same clay as that used in the production of their pots, and without the addition of a special ingredient or pigment, requires some explanation.

Due to the presence of iron (ferric oxide), Attic clay is normally red; but it can be changed to black and then back again to red by application of heat under certain conditions.

If fired in an *oxidizing fire* (i.e. with a strong draught providing plenty of oxygen), the clay remains *red* because the ferric oxide is unaffected.

The clay turns *black* in a reducing fire (i.e. when the fire is dampened, and the stoke-hole and vent of the kiln are closed, shutting off the supply of oxygen), because carbon monoxide (CO) is formed, which absorbs oxygen from the ferric oxide producing ferrous oxide, which is black ($CO + Fe_2O_3 = CO_2 + FeO$). The presence of water in the damp fuel complicates this chemical process, producing Fe_3O_4, an even blacker magnetic oxide of iron ($CO + 3Fe_2O_3 = CO_2 + Fe_3O_4$).

If the clay is *re-oxidized* by opening the stoke- and vent-holes, oxygen is re-absorbed and the red of ferric oxide restored.†

---

* Studies and experimentation in recent years as to possible techniques used by ancient Greek potters have concentrated on Attic clays and pottery.
† Thus the clay of a pot in cross-section may be fired:
    (1) *red throughout* (if oxidation is complete),
    (2) *black throughout* (if reduction is complete),
    (3) *black on the inner and outer edges of the cross-section and red in the centre*

Finally, a 'paint' made of Attic clay can be fired more intensely black
or red than a mass of clay, because a suspension of Attic clay in colloidal-sized particles contains a higher percentage of ferric oxide than
the paste of clay used in the production of pots. This is probably because
the very fine ferric oxide particles remain in suspension, while the less
fine non-ferric oxide particles are eliminated by sedimentation.

Due to the presence of silica and illite in Attic clay, it was possible for
the ancient potters to obtain a glossy finish. The ancient Greek kilns
were not sufficiently hot to fuse the silica into a true glaze, but at the
temperature attained (945° C.), the silica entered a transitional stage
known as sintering,* which provided a metallic lustre to the finished
surface. The illite contributed to the glossy finish because particles of
this mineral have a plate-like structure and tend, with evaporation, to
align themselves in the plane of any surface to which they are applied
in a thin coating (of colloidal-sized particles). The resultant coating is
smooth enough to reflect light.

MAKING THE POT

The steps in the production of pottery used by the ancient Greeks are
not known perfectly, but are surmised with considerable assurance as
follows:

Digging the clay from the clay pit.

Washing (i.e. mixing with water) and allowing it to settle in large pits
   to rid it of impurities–letting coarser and heavier particles settle
   out.

Ageing of the clay for perhaps six months, and '*ripening*' by mixing
   with it small quantities of older clay to increase bacterial action,
   and promote its working qualities.

Drying the clay to a paste of workable consistency.

Kneading, wedging and working the clay to make it smooth and to
   eliminate air bubbles.

Forming the pot:

   Centring a lump of clay on the potter's wheel, which is then spun
      and moulded (if too large to be formed in one operation, the pot
      was made in sections and joined later by a wet clay slip).

(if it was first oxidized and then partly reduced), or
   (4) *red on the inner and outer edges and black in the centre of the cross-section*
(if the second oxidation is incomplete).

---

* Sintering results in the production of a dense imporous coating even though actual
melting is not achieved.

Re-turning while the whole pot is semi-dry or of leather hardness and *cutting* to final shape with a knife.

Polishing with a damp cloth, leather or sponge.

Adding of handles and other adjuncts.

PAINTING THE POT

Essentially, the process of 'painting' consisted of covering the entire visible surface of the pot with a weak solution of the clay in suspension which was then allowed to dry. 'Painting' of the design followed, with strong concentrations being used for lines, figures and areas intended to contrast with the background in the final result. A somewhat less concentrated solution was employed for lines or areas intended to be less intense in final colour.

The colour of the surface prior to firing thus varied only in tone—according to the density and nature of the concentrations. The final contrasting red and black resulted from the firing, not from the addition of any special pigment.

Other colours used in pot painting included: (1) white, purple, yellow, grey, pink and a special red, all obtained by the use of white clay or ochre (alone, in various mixtures with each other, or in mixtures with the normal red clay) applied before firing, and owing their final colour at least in part to the firing process; (2) shades of blue, green, yellow, pink, purple and a matt black which were fugitive mineral or vegetable pigments applied after firing; (3) gold which was gold leaf applied before firing.

OTHER DECORATION

In contrast to the usual technique of 'painting' lines—using a dilute solution of paint and a brush—the *relief line*, a fine ridge of shiny black that can be felt with the finger, was developed to emphasize major details. This relief line was made with a very thick paste of 'paint', presumably extruded from an instrument similar to a fine syringe.

Incision was used to show the details of drawings. The incised line was made with a sharp pointed instrument before firing.

FIRING THE POT

For firing pots, the ancient Greeks used a kiln heated with wood or charcoal, and it appears almost certain that they used only one firing, though in one to three stages depending on the results desired. An initial oxidizing stage using heat of up to 800° C. was necessary in all cases for good firing of the pot. This stage left the pot red, deeper and more shiny on the parts 'painted' with the more concentrated solutions than on the other parts. The second stage of firing was reducing, produced by shutting off the supply of oxygen and dampening the fire by the introduction of damp fuel; at temperatures ranging from 800° C. to 945° C., with the presence of water vapour, this turned the entire pot black–again a deeper colour and more shiny on the areas painted with the more concentrated solutions. At the end of this stage, the kiln was cooled to about 875° C. In the third stage, the opening of the vent- and stoke-hole provided air for a re-oxidizing stage, the kiln being held for a time at 875° C. and then allowed to cool.

In this third stage the 'unpainted' and thinly 'painted' areas returned to the red of ferric oxide, while the thickly 'painted' areas remained black.*

VARIOUS TECHNIQUES AND TYPES OF POTTERY

Early Types of Painting: Proto-Geometric, Geometric and most of the early Archaic pottery was 'painted' with a concentrated solution and fired in three stages. Proto-Geometric and Geometric decoration was drawn with a compass and ruler or free-hand in straight lines. Apart from an occasional dotted design, such as a swastika, Proto-Geometric decorations were *solid*. In contrast, Geometric designs, though drawn in *outline* were usually hatched or cross-hatched; human and animal figures, when shown, were in solid silhouette. *Outline drawing* in dark 'paint' against a light background appeared in the early Archaic period. This technique is characteristic of Cycladic Linear Island pottery. 'Wild Goat' designers often used outline drawing with spotting or hatching for filling. Proto-Attic painters similarly used outline drawing, especially for human figures, though tending to complete major portions of their animals in solid silhouette. This resulted in the development of a *reserving technique* in which parts (usually the faces) of animals were drawn in outline and left in the background colour while the rest of the animal was done in solid silhouette. Proto-Attic, Laconian I, East Greek 'Wild Goat' and much Cycladic pottery is decorated in this technique.

Black Figure Technique: The Black Figure technique, developed in Attica in about 600 B.C., was 'painted' so that the figures and designs were presented against a red or orange-red background. In this technique, the whole vase was 'painted' with a film of weak concentration. After this weak concentration had dried, figures were 'painted' in

* See Joseph V. Noble, *op. cit.*, for a detailed description of this stage of firing.

silhouette in the strong concentration—sometimes a rough preliminary sketch made with a blunt instrument was followed. Then details were incised with a sharp point and ornaments 'painted' in the thick concentration. A subsequent three-stage firing (oxidizing, reducing and final re-oxidizing) left the thinly 'painted' background of the pot red, while the figures and designs which had been 'painted' in the thick solution remained black.

Red Figure Technique: The Red Figure technique also developed in Attica—in about 530 B.C. In this technique the background was black and the figures red. A rough preliminary sketch was made with a hard instrument directly on to the leather-hard surface of the clay. Next, the entire pot was coated with a light film of the weak concentration. After this had dried, the strong concentration was used to mark out carefully, with a broad thick outline, all areas finally to become black. These areas were then filled in with an even solution of the heavy concentration. Details of the figures were done with sharp relief lines in thick concentration, or with broader lines in a more dilute concentration if a final brown was intended. After painting, the pot went through the three-stage firing, which left the background, lines of detail and ornaments black, while the figures were reserved in red.

Attic White Ground: Attic white ground wares apparently went through the normal three firings. The Attic Red Figure White Ground pottery was 'painted' in the *outline technique.*

Black Painted or 'Black-Glazed' Wares: Black painted pottery required only two firings, the initial oxidizing firing and a subsequent reducing firing.

Bucchero: Bucchero ware is dark all the way through. It has a dilute very fine illite coating which gives it a faint sheen; but firing ended with the reducing stage, leaving the entire pot black.

Red Wares (Pergamene and Sigillata): Red wares—red throughout— were fired only once in an oxidizing fire. (These are typical of the Roman period.)

Other Wares: Certain Hellenistic wares, notably Hadra ware,* Canosa ware, and Centuripae ware, were apparently painted after firing (and whether there was then another firing appears doubtful).

Note: The greyness of potsherds often is the result of subsequent reduction, especially when pots were burnt on a funeral pyre.

CLAYS AND SLIPS

Clays, of course, varied from place to place, and even, from time to time, on one site.

* Some Hadra ware was ordinary Black Figure.

Slips (a thin coating of clay of a different constitution from that of the pot to which it is applied) also varied. Slips with a very low iron content fired to tones ranging from white to yellow; those with higher iron content gave a light brown, brownish or reddish colour in an oxidizing fire or black in a reducing fire.

Data relative to clays and slips is summarized in Appendix 3.

Part 3

PAINTING AND DESIGN
2800–146 B.C.

Identification
of More Important Designs
and Characteristics

A. Patterning of Designs

 Solid

 Scaled

 Checker or chessboard

 Dotted

 Hatched

 Drawn in outline

 Cross-hatched

 Incised (i.e. cut in)

 Latticed

B. More Important Designs

DESIGN	VARIATIONS	CHARACTERISTIC TYPE OR SCHOOL
1. *Cables*		
	Single colour	Proto-Attic
	Alternate colours	Proto-Attic
	Broken	Proto-Attic
	Single colour, solid centre	East Greek
	Broken	East Greek
	Rope	Cycladic
	Strand	Cycladic

DESIGN	VARIATIONS	CHARACTERISTIC TYPE OR SCHOOL
2. *Chevrons*		
	Reserved	Geometric
	Outline	Geometric
3. *Circles* (*and/or Semi-circles*)		
	Concentric, compass-drawn	Proto-Geometric
	Concentric, rough, heavy	Corinthian
	Concentric, rough, dotted	East Greek
4. *Eyes*		
	Simple circle and dot	Proto-Attic
	Frontal in profile face	Archaic (all types)
	Profile in profile face	Classical
5. *Lines*		
	Dotted	Laconian
	Heavy, wavy	Proto-Geometric
	Vertical, wavy	Proto-Corinthian
	Horizontal, wavy	Geometric, Proto-Attic
	Zig-zag	Geometric, Proto-Attic
	Horizontal parallel	Proto-Corinthian and 'Linear Island'
	Stepped	Proto-Attic, Chalcidian

DESIGN	VARIATIONS	CHARACTERISTIC TYPE OR SCHOOL
5. Lines (contd.)		
	Spirals, doubled	Proto-Attic
	Spiral, double	East Greek, Attic Black Figure and Red Figure
	Spiral, false	Geometric
	Lambda	Geometric
	Mu or 'm'	Geometric
	Nu or 'n'	Geometric
	'w'	Geometric
	Sigma	Geometric
	Running 's'	Geometric, Proto-Corinthian and Cycladic
	Alternating loops	Proto-Corinthian, East Greek
6. Lozenges		
	Solid	Proto-Attic, Cycladic, East Greek
	Cross-hatched	Proto-Geometric, Geometric
	Linked	Geometric, Proto-Corinthian
7. Meanders		
	Battlement	Proto-Geometric
	Hatched	Geometric, Cycladic
	Broken	East Greek, Laconian
	Broken	Proto-Attic
	Solid	Numerous variations in East Greek, Attic Black Figure and Red Figure

4

DESIGN	VARIATIONS	CHARACTERISTIC TYPE OR SCHOOL
8. *Plant Forms*		
	Ivy, leaf and berries	Attic Red Figure
	Ivy, doubled	Attic Black Figure
	Leaves	Proto-Attic
	Leaf cross or quatrefoil	Geometric, Cycladic
	Lotus flower and bud	East Greek
	Lotus buds, linked	Attic Black and Red Figure
	Palmette (variety of forms)	Throughout Archaic and Classical periods
	Pomegranate	Laconian
	Pomegranate net	Proto-Corinthian, Corinthian, Laconian
	Pomegranate, linked buds	Laconian
	Rays	All Archaic pottery
	Rosette, dot	Geometric, Proto-Attic
	Rosette, dot	East Greek
	Rosette, dot, stemmed	Proto-Corinthian
	Rosette, dot, stemmed	Proto-Attic
	Rosette, incised	Corinthian
	Rosette, incised	Corinthian, Early Attic, Chalcidian

DESIGN	VARIATIONS	CHARACTERISTIC TYPE OR SCHOOL
8. *Plant Forms* (*contd.*)		
	Rosette, outlined	Proto-Attic
	Rosette, 8-leaved	Proto-Corinthian
	Rosette, blobby	Proto-Corinthian
9. *Swastikas*		
	Solid	Geometric
	Dotted	Proto-Geometric
	Hatched	Geometric
	Hooked	Proto-Attic, East Greek
10. *Tongues*		
		Throughout Archaic
11. *Triangles*		
	Solid	Proto-Geometric, Geometric, Proto-Corinthian, Cycladic
	Cross-hatched	Geometric, Cycladic
	Solid-hooked or spiral hook	Proto-Attic
	Outline, hooked	East Greek
	Outline, pendant	East Greek
	Alternating, curved	Proto-Attic
	Opposed, or double axe	Geometric
	Opposed, or hourglass	Geometric

I Cretan Pottery (2800–1100 B.C.)

Cretan pottery is divided into three periods:

Early Minoan	2800–2000 B.C.
Middle Minoan	2000–1550 B.C.
Late Minoan	1550–1100 B.C.

It is pertinent to the present survey because Middle and Late Minoan pottery especially influenced Mycenaean pottery, which in turn had some influence on later Greek schools.

Middle Minoan pottery had a black background with designs painted in white and red. Middle Minoan I was made on a slow wheel; thereafter the pottery was made on a fast wheel. The pots were often coarse, though thin-walled.

Late Minoan pottery had a creamy buff background with designs painted in glossy orange, orange-red, red, brown and black. Characteristic designs included fish, octopus, nautilus shells, vines, leaves, and other flowing floral designs. Though made on a fast wheel, shapes were irregular and tended to be top-heavy.

II Helladic Pottery (2800–1100 B.C.)

Helladic pottery is divided into three main periods and the third period is sub-divided into three sub-periods:

Early Helladic	2800–1900 B.C.
Middle Helladic	1900–1550 B.C.
Late Helladic	1550–1100 B.C.
Mycenaean I	1550–1500 B.C.
Mycenaean II	1500–1425 B.C.
Mycenaean III	1425–1100 B.C.

Helladic pottery influenced sub-Mycenaean pottery, but stands in strong contrast to Geometric. Later stages of Helladic pottery are thus worthy of brief note.

Background: Middle Helladic: buff; Late Helladic: creamy buff.

Colour of Designs: Middle Helladic: matt (dull) black; Late Helladic: glossy red, red-orange, brown, black.

Decoration: The Mycenaean potters of the Late Helladic period conceived their pots as single wholes, hence the decoration embraced the whole pot. The decoration was characterized by flowing lines and stripes. Drawing was free-spreading, but lacked understanding of subtleties of curve and spacing.

Repertory of Designs: Free-hand concentric semi-circles, and concentric circles, wavy lines, chequers, joined spirals, symbolic floral designs, symbolic birds and animals (and sometimes humans).

III 'Sub-Mycenaean' Pottery (1100–1050 B.C.)

Between the end of the Helladic period proper and the appearance of true Greek pottery, the pottery degenerated. Pottery from this period is sometimes known as 'Sub-Mycenaean' or Mycenaean-type pottery.

Decoration: It is characterized by a lifeless, limited repertory of simple ornaments arranged in bands, with one broad band around the main girth of the pot, and narrow bands (often three of them) above and below.

Repertory of Designs: Free-hand spirals, concentric arcs, and meaningless and stylized floral designs.

Shapes of Pots: Crude and sagging.

IV Proto-Geometric Pottery (1050–900 B.C.)

Origins: Proto-Geometric was widespread, being made in Attica, the Peloponnese, Boeotia, probably the Ionian Islands, the Cyclades, Rhodes, and Cos; it was also made in Thessaly and Macedonia. The Attic was the best and dominated the field.

Background: Reddish-brown to dark brown and black. Large pots were light in background. Small vessels often had a dark background except in the area of decorated panels.

Colour of Designs: Black or brown.

Decoration: Broad contrasts of dark and light (with initial emphasis of design on the shoulder and the field between the handles) were characteristic (later emphasis shifted to the main body).

Repertory of Designs: Compass-drawn concentric circles and concentric semi-circles with or without a central dot or solid core; lozenges (diamonds), chequers, hourglasses, swastikas, triangles, and vertical zig-zags in one or more horizontal bands, cross-hatched or solid designs. The meander (or key) was *rare* and not hatched–the 'battlement' meander appearing among late Proto-Geometric designs. No men or animals, except an occasional horse done in silhouette with a few quick strokes.

Shapes of Pots: Contours crisp, neat and taut. Tall oval body, low centre of gravity. High foot. Made by hand on a rapid wheel.

Clay: Pale to mid-brown, sometimes gritty.

Typical Proto-Geometric Designs 1050–900 B.C.

Fig. 1
Concentric circles
1050–900 B.C.

Fig. 2
Concentric
semi-circles
1050–900 B.C.

Fig. 3
Concentric
semi-circles
with solid cores
1050–900 B.C.

Typical Proto-Geometric Designs 1050–900 B.C. (*contd.*)

Fig. 4
Concentric
semi-circles with
'hourglass' or
opposed triangles
1050–900 B.C.

Fig. 5
Cross-hatching
950–900 B.C.

Fig. 6
Chequer design
950–900 B.C.

Fig. 7
Lozenges
cross-hatched and chequered
950–900 B.C.

Typical Proto-Geometric Designs 1050–900 B.C. (*contd.*)

Fig. 8
Wavy lines and
other designs
950–900 B.C.

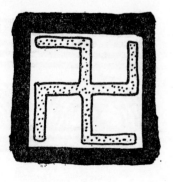

Fig. 9
Dotted swastika
(see Fig. 15 for
contrast with
Geometric swastika)
c. 900 B.C.

Fig. 10
Band design
c. 900 B.C.

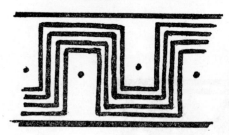

Fig. 11
Battlement meander
(see Figs. 12–14 for hatched
Geometric meanders)
Late Proto-Geometric–
Early Geometric

V Geometric Pottery (900–700 B.C.)

Origins: Geometric was above all an Attic–and Athenian–style. Geometric pottery was also produced in Argos, Corinth, Boeotia, Thessaly, Ithaca, Euboea, the Cyclades, Laconia, Rhodes, Cos, Crete, the East Greek cities of Asia Minor, Etruria, Sicily and South Italy. It was primarily an urban rather than a rural or peasant style.

EARLY GEOMETRIC (900–850 B.C.)
Colour of Background: Reddish-brown.
Colours of Designs: Dark brown to black. White rarely, for subordinate designs.
Decoration: The whole surface of the pot was decorated with abstract geometric designs in a series of horizontal bands, some divided into square frames. The emphasis of the design was on the belly and neck.
Repertory of Designs: The meander (or 'key': drawn with two fine lines of outline, the space between being filled with diagonal hatching) was characteristic of the period. Other designs included: concentric circles (though dying out), chequers, triangles, rows of oblique strokes and sets of horizontal zig-zags. There were *no* semi-circles or human figures or animals (except occasional birds).
Shapes of Pots: Clearly defined (emphasized by decoration and design), low foot, slim body, high narrow neck, strong handles.
Clay: Medium clear brown, fairly fine.

MATURE GEOMETRIC (850–730 B.C.)
Colour of Background: Reddish-brown: often with a pale slip.
Colour of Designs: Dark brown and black: often with a sheen.
Decoration: Whereas Early Geometric designs literally covered almost every available space, Mature Geometric left more open space as plain background. Two tendencies appeared:
  (1) Continual lightening of the dark tone by inserting more bands of ornaments, and
  (2) Revival of the system of panels (not used since Proto-Geometric).
Repertory of Designs: The hatched meander remained characteristic. Other designs included: quatrefoils (four-leafed ornament), swastikas, rows of triangles and chains of lozenges (diamonds). Figures of animals including deer, horses and goats appeared in the 8th century and birds a little later. These were drawn in full silhouette in rows of repeated patterns. People were in profile silhouette with triangular chests and match-stick arms held in a triangle or a square over their heads; their legs were a bit more rounded and shaped. Scenes showed

chariots (with two wheels side by side, the car unattached, and the driver in the air), funeral scenes (the body on the bier would be a horizontally turned figure, and the scene a mere inventory of items).
Shapes of Pots: The transition from neck to body was sharply articulated (where slurred previously); proportions were carefully harmonized; pots were often very large.
Clay: Medium clear brown, fairly fine.

LATE GEOMETRIC (730–700 B.C.)

Colour of Background: Pale clay.
Colour of Designs: Dark brown and black (sometimes the dark outline was filled with light brown or white). Strong sheen.
Decorations: Decoration was rich, often with broad panels divided into vertical strips. Intervals between figures were filled with a shimmering background of zig-zags. Increasingly more open space was left free. Figures appeared in two zones which occupied most of the vase. Legendary scenes began to appear for the first time.
Repertory of Designs: Meanders, chequers, chevrons, cross-hatched batons, simple stripes varied with zig-zag lines with drip marks at nadir, and spirals at the base and near handles (first appearance).
Men, animals and *birds:* the faces of animals and men were white; the figures were rather thin, but rounded and curved; humans were no longer mere silhouettes or triangular chested symbols. Chariots, when shown, were in silhouette with only one wheel seen; the driver rested on the chariot. Birds appeared in a band of silhouettes punctuated by dots.
Shapes of Pots: Plastic snakes often appeared on handles, shoulders, and lips.
Clay: Fine, brown.

ARGIVE GEOMETRIC (900–700 B.C.)

Argive Geometric pottery, produced primarily at Argos but also at Tiryns, Asine and Argive Heraeum, while far less important than Attic Geometric was, nevertheless, the second most important Geometric school and deserves brief mention.
Background: Same as Attic.
Colour of Designs: Characteristically, a broad panel framed with vertical strips and located between the handles of the pot constituted the main field. The rest of the pot was covered by both wide and narrow bands of ornaments and striping. The general effect was heavy and lumpish.
Repertory of Designs: Usual Attic Geometric designs were common plus the step meander, and massed horizontal and vertical zig-zags. In figure scenes, horses were common, sometimes in pairs with a man

or a manger between. Women often had long strings hanging from the front of their skirts.

Shapes of Pots: Well made.

Clay: Sometimes greenish.

Note: No Argive style of importance developed after the Geometric period. An *Argive Sub-Geometric* style with orientalizing influence, and animals with solid heads and outline faces, developed briefly (700–650 B.C.), but disappeared in the face of Corinthian competition. An *Argive Monochrome* style also reached its height in the 7th century. It was pale and unpainted, its decoration being composed of incised or pricked zig-zags and wavy lines. These wares were made by hand (not on a wheel) of a putty-coloured clay.

For other Proto-Geometric and Geometric pottery, see Appendix 1, I.

Typical Geometric Designs 900–700 B.C.

Fig. 12
'Greek key' or, more correctly, meander. (Note hatching in contrast to lack of hatching in Proto-Geometric meander of Fig. 11) 900–800 B.C.

Fig. 13
Step meander
800–700 B.C.

Fig. 14
Variety of Fig. 13
800–700 B.C.

Fig. 15
Swastika. (Note hatching
in contrast to Fig. 9)

Fig. 16
Quatrefoil
8th century B.C.

Typical Geometric Designs 900–700 B.C. (*contd.*)

Fig. 17
Cross-hatched triangles
8th century B.C.

Fig. 18
Cross-hatched triangles
and dotted lozenges
8th century B.C.

Fig. 19
Cross-hatched triangles,
lozenges, etc.
8th century B.C.

Fig. 20
Wavy lines with drip
marks at nadir
8th century B.C.

Fig. 21
Wavy lines
8th century B.C.

Fig. 22
Types of chevrons
9th and 8th centuries B.C.

Fig. 23
Human
figure,
wavy lines,
chequer, etc.
8th century
B.C.

Fig. 24
Birds,
triangles,
lozenges, etc.
8th century
B.C.

Fig. 25
Horse, bird,
wavy lines,
lozenges, etc.
8th century
B.C.

Fig. 26
Deer,
triangles,
chequers, etc.
8th century
B.C.

Typical Corinthian Geometric Designs 900–700 B.C.*

Fig. 27
Corinthian Geometric
birds and wavy lines:
note use of parallel lines
800–750 B.C.

Fig. 28
Corinthian Geometric
cross-hatched triangles
and dotted lozenges:
note again heavy use
of parallel lines
800–750 B.C.

* See Appendix 1, I.

VI Archaic Pottery (700–480 B.C.)

GENERAL

Towards the end of the 8th century B.C., contact with the East brought an orientalizing influence in Greek vase painting. The rigid angles and lines of the Geometric style were replaced by curved and flowing lines. New shapes, patterns and designs appeared, including plant forms, and animal and fanciful designs.

The date of 700 B.C. for the end of the Geometric period and the beginning of the Archaic period is, of course, arbitrary. Some pots showing evidence of the new style appeared before that date, and other pots in the old style continued to be produced. Often it is difficult to say with precision whether a particular pot is Late Geometric or Early Archaic. Proto-Corinthian, Proto-Attic and other early Archaic pottery retained many features and designs from Late Geometric. Within a few years, however, the change was clearly evident in totally new styles featuring animals, people, and plant forms and a considerable modification of even those old designs like the meander that were retained. Cycladic and East Greek pottery of the Archaic period made much use of cross-hatching on triangles and birds, hatched meanders and the like, but these were drawn with far less precision and have little resemblance to their Geometric counterparts.

The orientalizing influence was adopted most readily by the potters and painters of Corinth, whose products, painted in the 'Animal Style', dominated the Greek market until about 550 B.C. At this point Attic vase painters adapted the human form to vase painting and ended the Corinthian dominance. Other important Archaic styles include Laconian, Cycladic, and East Greek, each of which is clearly distinguishable.

CORINTH*

PROTO-CORINTHIAN (*c. 725–c. 625 B.C.*)
  Background: Pale buff.
  Colour of Designs: Black with some other colours added for lesser features. Later purple was used more with brown, yellow and white for details.
  Decoration: Under an orientalizing influence, the Geometric Style

---

* Those desiring greater detail on Corinthian styles are referred to Appendix 1, II.

was modified by new shapes and patterns. At first, the style was mixed with geometric patterns (often on the neck) appearing alongside the new black painted figure designs (often on the body). Later (after 700 B.C.), the geometric features were replaced by the incised Black Figure technique using heavily engraved lines, and the friezes were divided by two or three narrow lines.

Repertory of Designs: At first symbolic plant forms included hooked spirals, coronas of leaves, cables, rings of solid triangles, volutes, rosettes, and a few animal and bird figures (which were curved, had eyes and white faces and were capable of movement), including horses, lions, cocks, etc. Later (after 700 B.C.), animal figures predominated: the Hittite lion, sphinxes (usually in facing pairs), dogs, horses and birds (usually in files), and goats and centaurs. Plant forms used for decoration were symbolic, with chains of lotus flowers and buds, palmettes, and stalked dot rosettes being added to the repertory. Human figures, bearded gods and warriors also appeared, but less frequently than animals. The figures were drawn boldly with full rounded forms and in vigorous tense positions.

Shapes of Pots: Small, neat and precise.

Clay: Fine whitish clay fired to pinkish tinge.

CORINTHIAN ANIMAL STYLE (*c.* 625–*c.* 550 B.C.)

Background: Pale buff. At the end of the period an orange slip was added to the main panels to imitate the Attic style.

Colour of Designs: Black with numerous other colours, notably purple with yellow and white for details; tendency to greater use of colours.

Decoration: Based on animals, it quickly became cheap, pretentious and mass-produced with a tendency for the animals to become larger and more elongated, and eventually wooden and lumpy. The use of incision and additional colours also increased. Broad black bands (to separate the friezes) replaced the earlier thin lines.

Repertory of Designs: Panther* and Assyrian lion (replacing Hittite lion) often in facing pairs or on either side of a third animal (bull, etc.). At the height of this style (625–600 B.C.) the repertory of animals was very large: it included boars, bulls, goats, deer, hares, eagles, geese, owls, cocks, snakes and many weird creatures such as sphinxes, griffins, gorgons, and humans with wings, and snake, fish or animal bodies. After 600 B.C. the repertory shrank and figures became emaciated and perfunctorily drawn. Plant and other decorations tended to become more dense and included tongues, scale designs, double and quadruple lotuses, lotus palmette crosses, dots, etc. The stalked dot rosette degenerated to a blobby solid incised shape.

* In archaeological jargon, a lion-like beast is known as a 'panther' when rendered full-face and a 'lion' when the head is in profile.

Shapes of Pots: Though small ware continued in use, there was a tendency to use larger forms.

Clay: Fine whitish clay fired to a greenish tinge.

Note: Along with the fine pottery of the Proto-Corinthian and Animal Styles, there was also some human figure pottery–which, however, never attained the perfection of the Animal Style. There also continued to exist in Corinth cheaper pottery, first of Sub-Geometric Style, then developing into a simple linear style and a simple white style for common usage.

Typical Archaic Corinthian Designs

1. PROTO-CORINTHIAN: 725–625 B.C.

    (Note extensive use of parallel lines, relative simplicity, and use of stylized plant forms.)

Fig. 29
Alternating loops,
parallel lines
and base rays
c. 700 B.C.

Fig. 30
Dotted lozenges
and parallel lines
c. 700 B.C.

Fig. 31
Parallel lines
and wavy lines
700–675 B.C.

Typical Archaic Corinthian Designs (*contd.*)

1. PROTO-CORINTHIAN: 725–625 B.C. (*contd.*)

Fig. 32
Open cable, meander,
bird and parallel lines
c. 700 B.C.

Fig. 33
Rosette and
parallel lines
c. 700 B.C.

Fig. 34
Base rays
675–650 B.C.

Fig. 35
Stalked dot rosettes,
parallel lines and
zig-zags
675–650 B.C.

Fig. 36
Stalked dot rosette
and zig-zag or 'sigma'
design
675–650 B.C.

Typical Archaic Corinthian Designs (*contd.*)

1. PROTO-CORINTHIAN: 725–625 B.C. (*contd.*)

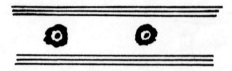

Fig. 37
Rosettes and parallel lines
675–650 B.C.

2. CORINTHIAN ANIMAL STYLE: 625–550 B.C.
A. *Early Animal Style.*

Fig. 38
Dog: note dot
rosettes with stalks
to right of animal
675–650 B.C.

B. *Mature and Late Animal Styles*

Fig. 39
Winged panthers:
note degeneration
of rosette to mere
blob with incised
divisions
c. 600 B.C.

Typical Archaic Corinthian Designs (*contd.*)

2. CORINTHIAN ANIMAL STYLE: 625–550 B.C. (*contd.*)

Fig. 40
Snake-headed bird
with blob rosettes
600–575 B.C.

Fig. 41
Sphinx,
degenerated rosettes
600–570 B.C.

Fig. 42
Panther
600–550 B.C.

LACONIA*

After Attica and Corinth, Laconia was the third most important mainland producer of pottery during the Archaic period.†

LACONIAN I (RESERVING PERIOD) (700–630 B.C.)
  Background: Light, often with a slip.

* For greater detail, see Appendix 1. II.
† Laconian pottery is sometimes known erroneously as 'Cyrenaic' because it was first found at Cyrene.

Colour of Designs: Dark, black, with purple or white for details.

Decoration: The early Archaic pottery of Laconia was decorated in a negligent and extremely simple style, conservative and restrained, using linear and abstract patterns, and broad bands of dark paint with little filling ornament. Animals appeared late and were in solid silhouette with reserved faces.

Repertory of Designs: The commonest and most characteristic designs included a row of squares set between two rows of dots around the rim of the pot, broad painted areas and bands of purple. Other designs included: chequers, and other solid ornaments, broken and unbroken cables, rosettes (sometimes reserved against dark background), tongues, rays, rows of pomegranates, spirals, hollow squares with a dot in the centre, clumsy palmettes. Animals, human figures and heads set in panels were rare—when shown, they had little or no body detail while heads were large and reserved: and sometimes patches of purple or white were added.

Shapes of Pots: The shapes had individuality embodying ridges and angles that interrupted the smooth curve of the contours (sometimes with plastic heads).

Clay: Similar to Attic, but darker and varying to coarser and pink.

LACONIAN II (EARLY BLACK FIGURE) (630–590 B.C.)

Background: Light.

Colour of Designs: Black figure, free use of purple.

Decoration: Decoration was still simple with little ornament to relieve the plain banding. Birds were the most characteristic figures (more often used than animals: human figures were rare). At first incision only followed the outline of figures. Patches of purple were later used more for details. Little filling ornament was used.

Repertory of Designs: Broad bands of colour, silhouette birds with drooping purple tails, animals and monsters copied from Corinthian, rows of squares between two rows of dots (squares more widely spaced than in Laconian I), rays and double rays, variations of step and hook meander, chevrons, tongues, cables, pomegranates (shaped like balls with spikes through them), rosettes.

Shapes of Pots: Pronounced ring foot, outcurving walls, ridges, grooves, knobs, plastic heads, strong angles, bold curves all common.

Clay: Same as Laconian I.

LACONIAN III AND IV (DEVELOPED BLACK FIGURE STYLE) (590–550 and 550–525 B.C.)

Background: Light: creamy slip (sometimes areas were left unslipped).

Colour of Designs: Deep sepia to black, free use of purple.

Decoration: Style was restrained, honest and simple. Incision was used with economy. Though imitative of Corinthian painting, Laconian remained strongly individualistic.

Repertory of Designs: Animal and human figures drawn from mythology and daily life, little filling ornaments, buildings and bushes (common), winged boys and birds, grubbing cocks, pomegranates (shaped like balls with numerous stamens and often a cross bar), continuous bands of stylized, elongated and even spindly lotuses and buds, tapering myrtle leaves (with or without stems or stalks) and ivy, palmettes, hooked meander, "Σ"-shaped bracket.

Shapes of Pots: Cups were a favourite shape. Plastic palmettes, and heads, copies of bronze pot details (i.e. rivet heads, etc.) were common relief features.

Clay: Less fine than Attic or Corinthian, fired to colours ranging from pink to light brown.

LACONIAN PLAIN WARE (600–500 B.C.)

Decoration: Also produced were pots decorated with a simple linear pattern, sometimes with the upper half dark and the lower covered with a creamy slip; sometimes a purple band appeared at the belly with white lines enclosing dots above and below.

Typical Archaic Laconian Designs 700–500 B.C.

Fig. 43
Laconian lions
c. 650 B.C.

(after a photograph by E. A. Lane)

Fig. 44
Squares between
dotted lines
c. 650 B.C.

(based on an illustration from R. M. Cook's Greek Painted Pottery, *Methuen, and reproduced with their kind permission)*

Typical Archaic Laconian Designs 700–500 B.C. (*contd.*)

Fig. 45
Droop-tailed birds,
squares between dotted
lines, parallel lines
c. 600 B.C.

Fig. 46
Elaborate palmette
600–525 B.C.

Fig. 47
Droop-tailed bird
c. 540 B.C.

Fig. 48
Pomegranates, leaves,
tongues and parallel lines
c. 540 B.C.

THE CYCLADES*

Various Cycladic styles exist. Their origins are disputed. There are variations relative to the colours used for the background and the designs, and to the clay. Certain generalizations, however, may be made with regard to Cycladic pottery of the Archaic period:

Background: Light: often a yellowish or creamy slip.

* For greater detail, see Appendix 1, III.

Colour of Designs: Dark; black and browns predominated (except on 'Melian' which also used purple and light brown); finish varied from shiny to dull.

Decoration: In general, Cycladic pottery was painted broadly with the brush alone (not incised) with the aim of portraying lively movement rather than anatomical structure. Animals usually had reserved (i.e. outlined) white faces with eyes, while their bodies were solid, dotted or chequered. Emphasis usually was on the neck and shoulders of the pot (except on 'Melian' where it was on the body of the pot).

Repertory of Designs: Animals (wiry and boneless) included deer, lions, dancing lions, winged, wingless or dancing horses, griffins, sphinxes, heads or foreparts of animals, humans and little birds. Floral and other designs included lotuses and floral chains, hatched meanders, thick wavy lines, horizontal, vertical, solid, hatched and dotted zig-zags, false and simple spirals, concentric circles flanked by four dots, thick circles containing eight leaved stars or discs, rows of dots, spiked dots, large round dots, S-shaped blobs, tall blobs, cross-hatched lozenges and triangles, large lozenges with extra corners, opposed or boxed triangles, chequers, chevrons, latticing, quatrefoils, narrow stripes, curvilinear lines, simple cables, rays and reversed rays.

Shapes of Pots: Varied widely from thick to thin and included all shapes.

Clay: Varied widely from red to brown and yellow-brown, and from fine to coarse, with micaceous and volcanic impurities according to the local source.

Typical Archaic Cycladic Designs 700–480 B.C.

A. THERAN SUB-GEOMETRIC (see Appendix 1, III:1)

Fig. 49
Hatched zig-zag lines
and cross-hatched squares,
tied concentric circles
700–675 B.C.

Fig. 50
Cross-hatched triangles
and bird
700–675 B.C.

Typical Archaic Cycladic Designs 700–480 B.C. (*contd.*)

Fig. 51
Hatched wheel rosette,
cross-hatched triangles,
tied concentric circles
700–675 B.C.

Fig. 52
Solid triangle with
spirals and parallel
lines
700–675 B.C.

B. 'Linear Island Group' (see Appendix 1, III:3) *c.* 750–650 B.C.

Fig. 53
Dotted lion: note reserved
face and use of parallel lines
700–675 B.C.

Fig. 54
Horse, cross-hatched
triangles, cable and
hatched meander:
note reserved face
700–650 B.C.

Typical Archaic Cycladic Designs 700–480 B.C. (*contd.*)

C. 'AD GROUP' (see Appendix 1, III:4) *c.* 700–675 B.C.

Fig. 55
Winged horse, wavy lines, solid lozenges and triangles 700–675 B.C.
(*based on an illustration from the* Berliner Jahrbuch, *and reproduced by kind permission of Gebr. Mann Verlag, Berlin*)

D. 'HERALDIC GROUP' (see Appendix 1, III:5) *c.* 700–650 B.C.

Fig. 56
Note heraldic position of the two lions, reserved faces, broken cable, solid lozenges, triangles, etc. 700–650 B.C.

E. 'PROTOME GROUP' (characterized by cut-off forepart or head of an animal: see Appendix 1, III:6) 675–625 B.C.

Fig. 57
Note reserved face of lion and stylized plant form on right *c.* 650 B.C.

(*Figs. 57 and 58 are based on illustrations from R. M. Cook's* Greek Painted Pottery, *Methuen, and reproduced with their kind permission*)

Fig. 58
Similar comment *c.* 650 B.C.

EAST GREEK STYLES*

The Greek cities of Asia Minor and the nearby islands (i.e. Lesbos, Samos, Cos, Chios, Rhodes, etc.) produced various styles of pottery known generally as East Greek. This region produced pottery from the Proto-Geometric to the Geometric and Archaic and even later periods. Of chief interest is the so-called 'Wild Goat' Style characteristic of Rhodes, which influenced pottery styles of the entire region.

EAST GREEK 'WILD GOAT' STYLE (650–500 B.C.)
Background: Cream: pale slip or wash.
Colour of Designs: Dark brown with some purple and white, not shiny.
Decoration: Draughtsmanship was careless and apparently spontaneous in reserved (i.e. brush-stroke outline) technique; brushwork was thick and rough. Filling ornaments were light and well scattered.
Repertory of Designs: The 'wild goat' was characteristic; other animals included: spotted deer, lion, griffin, sphinx, dogs chasing hares, boar, bull, swallows, geese, swans, etc. Other designs included: the meander, rosette, cable, square, rays, lotus flowers and buds, leaves, tongues, pendant triangles, freehand concentric semi-circles, and circles, dotted circles, etc. These designs appeared in outline on earlier pottery but often were solid on later pottery.
Shapes of Pots: Varied.
Clay: Coarse and gritty, usually fired from sandy brown to pink, but sometimes chocolate to salmon-red.

OTHER EAST GREEK STYLES
1. Grey Ware (or Bucchero): Geometric to Archaic, from Lesbos; unpainted grey pottery with ridges and incised or impressed decoration including hatched meanders and triangles.
2. East Greek Bowls: Archaic; bird bowls, rosette bowls, lotus bowls, eye bowls (named after the typical design).
3. Chiot Chalices: 600–550 B.C., from Chios; fine, thin-walled chalices (and phialai) decorated with human and animal figures.
4. Ionian Little Master Cups: 560–510 B.C., probably from Samos. finely made and well decorated cups in Black Figure technique on reddish ground with details of design either incised or very finely reserved. The interiors were usually decorated with concentric circles spreading out from the centre to the rim.

---

* For greater detail on East Greek pottery, Proto-Geometric to Late Archaic, see Appendix 1, IV.

5. Fikellura: 575–500 B.C., from Rhodes and Samos; animal and human figures as well as fanciful creatures in full silhouette, with details reserved.

6. Clazomenian: 550–525 B.C., from Clazomenae; Black Figure human and animal figures.

7. Vroulian Cups: 600–525 B.C., from Rhodes; light colours on black background, thin-walled cups.

8. Black Figure: 600–525 B.C.; tended to avoid use of incision (details were reserved) with the result that the effect was simple but somewhat blobby.

9. Banded Ware: 700–480 B.C., found throughout the area; cheap, common ware with simple banded design.

Typical Archaic East Greek Designs 700–500 B.C.

A. 'WILD GOAT' STYLE 650–500 B.C. Development of the lotus flower and bud.

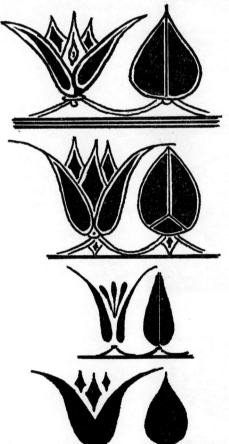

Fig. 59
650–625 B.C.

Fig. 60
630–600 B.C.

(*Figs. 60–63 are based on illustrations from R. M. Cook's* Greek Painted Pottery, *Methuen, and reproduced with their kind permission*)

Fig. 61
615–600 B.C.

Fig. 62
600–575 B.C.

Typical Archaic East Greek Designs 700–500 B.C. (*contd.*)

A. 'WILD GOAT' STYLE (*contd.*)

Fig. 63
600–575 B.C.
Note: See also Fig. 80

Fig. 64
Tongues, palmette,
early type goat,
broken cable
675–650 B.C.

Fig. 65
Pendant and upright
triangles, hooked
swastika, concentric
semi-circle,
'Wild Goat' Style A
650–625 B.C.

Fig. 66
Similar designs featuring
a goose
650–625 B.C.

Typical Archaic East Greek Designs 700–500 B.C. (*contd.*)

A. 'WILD GOAT' STYLE (*contd.*)

Fig. 67
Cable design
650–625 B.C.

Fig. 68
Hooked swastika,
dot rosette,
stalked rosette, bird
650–625 B.C.

Fig. 69
Typical of 'Wild Goat'
Style A
625–600 B.C.

Fig. 70
As above
625–600 B.C.

Fig. 71
Typical
'Wild Goat' Style
c. 600 B.C.

Typical Archaic East Greek Designs 700–500 B.C. (*contd.*)

B. CHIOT STYLE 700–550 B.C. (see Appendix 1, IV:4)

Fig. 72
Chiot bird, pendant
triangle, concentric
circles, etc.
625–600 B.C.

Fig. 73
Chiot bull and bird,
pendant semi-circles,
triangles, etc.
625–600 B.C.

Fig. 74
Base of Chiot chalice
showing typical
placement of design
600–575 B.C.
(*after A. de Longpérier,*
Musée Napoléon *III,*
plate 52)

C. IONIAN 'LITTLE MASTERS' STYLE *c.* 550 B.C.
   (see Appendix 1, IV:5)

Fig. 75
Typical use of ivy or
double myrtle branches
and leaves
c. 550 B.C.

Typical Archaic East Greek Designs 700–500 B.C. (*contd.*)

D. BIRD BOWL STYLE 700–600 B.C. (see Appendix 1, IV:1)

Fig. 76
Cross-hatched bird,
pendant triangle,
and lozenge
700–650 B.C.

E. FIKELLURA STYLE 575–500 B.C.

Fig. 77
Bird, spirals,
stylized flowers
c. 540 B.C.

Fig. 78
Curved arcs
c. 540 B.C.

(*Figs. 77 and 78 are based on Fig. 25 in*
J. Boehlen's Aus ionischen und italischen Nekropolen)

Fig. 79
Fikellura human
c. 525 B.C.

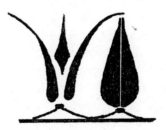

Fig. 80
Fikellura lotus flower
and bud
550–525 B.C.

(*Figs. 79 and 80 are based on illustrations from*
R. M. Cook's Greek Painted Pottery, Methuen,
and reproduced with their kind permission)

Typical Archaic East Greek Designs 700–500 B.C. (*contd.*)

F. CYPRIOT STYLE*

Fig. 81
Cypriot bird and lotus plant
700–600 B.C.

ATTICA†

PROTO-ATTIC (*c.* 710–*c.* 610 B.C.)

Background: Light buff or yellowish slip.

Colour of Designs: Dark, including black and purple with considerable white and yellowish-white, especially in early and middle periods (i.e. until about 650 B.C.), but with less white thereafter. Briefly (i.e. for a brief period), reds, yellow, browns, and bluish-green were employed in the Late Proto-Attic period. The tendency was clearly towards use of black as the main colour for designs.

Decoration: Decoration developed from an early mixture of Geometric with the Orientalizing Style of animals and flowing lines towards Black Figure silhouette. Animals and humans became the main subjects. Animals quickly became common in black silhouette with reserved faces and details incised or painted in purple or white. Humans were done in outline technique for a longer period, with details (often purple faces) painted in black, purple or white. Decoration was large and heavy; at first it was not well planned or balanced; figures were ill-proportioned and unequal in size; later, planning and execution improved. The whole pot (even including under its handles) was regarded as one unbroken field for decoration. Scenes were often mythological.

Repertory of Designs: Animals included: lions, panthers, horses,

---

* The Cypriot Style in fact differs markedly from the other East Greek styles. It is included here for the sake of convenience.
† For greater detail, see Appendix 1, V.

gorgons, dogs, cocks, eagles and other birds. Floral and other designs included: solid rays, double spirals, lozenges with spiral hooks, heart-shaped pairs of spirals, hooks, spotted leaves, palmettes, horizontal zig-zags, cables, rosettes, floral chains, mill sail patterns, oblique meanders, dot and incised rosettes.

Shapes of Pots: Pots tended to be slim but large and with simple sturdy contours.

Clay: Pale and coarse.

BLACK FIGURE (*c.* 610–*c.* 480 B.C.)

Background: Orange-red.

Colour of Designs: Shiny black with purple and white for details (infrequently other colours were also used).

Decoration: At first, decoration was 'narrative' showing mythological scenes in narrow bands arranged in horizontal tiers encircling the pot; style was meticulous in detail and in use of titles to identify the characters. Men were painted in black, women in white. Human figures were depicted with frontal upper body and lower body in profile. The face was in profile–with, however, a frontal eye. Animals not in the main scenes were presented in perfunctory rows on the rim or lower parts of the pot.

Later, decoration concentrated on a single large field framed by bands of decoration. Depiction of 'mood' replaced the narrative as the scene concentrated on the moment of crisis in the mythological story. Drawing of human figures became larger and more attention was given to anatomy. Subsidiary ornament became sparser.

After introduction of the 'Red Figure' technique, in about 530 B.C., this new technique influenced the Black Figure technique: all participants in scenes tended to act as on a stage; scenes tended to show everyday life rather than portray heroic grandeur; composition and detail became fussy.

In general, except during the Late Black Figure period, the style was severe, austere, dignified, sombre and even grim.

Repertory of Designs: Subjects shown included gods, heroes and men in mythological scenes with such other objects (ships, chariots, animals or mythological creatures) as were necessary to the situation.

On Early Black Figure pots, bands of animal friezes occupied important parts of the pots showing horses, boars, lions, panthers, dogs, hares, etc. Floral and other designs included lotus buds and flowers, palmettes, bands of dots, chequers, tongues and rays.

Later, subsidiary designs of all types lost their importance; narrow bands of lotus and palmettes or meanders were used for frames, and rays were used on the base; elsewhere such designs were used sparingly.

6

Shapes of Pots: Shapes of pots varied widely, tending generally to medium-sized and small fine vessels. Cups were of special interest and various beautiful shapes were developed. Amphorae also were of special interest, particularly the Panathenaic Amphorae.

Clay: Fine, orange-red.

Note: For the first time, in early 6th century pottery, the potters and painters can be identified either by their signatures on the pots or by their styles.

RED FIGURE (*c.* 530–*c.* 480 B.C.)

Background: Shiny black.

Colour of Designs: Orange-red (purple used decreasingly for beard and hair).

Decoration: Mythological scenes were gradually replaced by scenes of human life. Other decoration tended to be scarce. Figures of humans became supple, in natural poses with torso in profile, full or three-quarters view. The profile eye began to replace the full eye. More attention was given to folds and fit of dress.

Repertory of Designs: Apart from the human figures shown in the main panel, ornamentation was scarce; it included lotus and palmette chains and simple meanders.

Shapes of Pots: Pots were simple, rhythmically designed and finely executed. The single-curve cup became the most popular form.

Clay: Orange-red and fine.

WHITE GROUND POTTERY

Near the end of the 6th century B.C. a white background was introduced for use in the Black Figure technique. Similarly, white ground was also used for the Red Figure technique. In general, the white ground was used on lekythoi and for other funeral vases.

BLACK PAINTED POTTERY or 'BLACK-GLAZED WARE'
(550–480 B.C.)

Pottery covered simply with plain black paint appeared in the Late Archaic period. Early examples are rare and have little artistic merit. In the 5th century B.C., however, this pottery was beautifully shaped, covered with a shiny black, and made of fine clay.

Typical Archaic Attic Designs

1. PROTO-ATTIC: 710–610 B.C.

Fig. 82
Lozenges with spiral hooks
c. 705 B.C.

Fig. 83
Double spiral
c. 705 B.C.

Fig. 84
Spotted leaves
700–680 B.C.

Fig. 85
Lozenge with
extra points
700–680 B.C.

Fig. 86
Hooked solid rays
700–680 B.C.

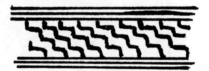

Fig. 87
Step zig-zag
700–680 B.C.

Fig. 88
Flower design
675–650 B.C.

Fig. 89
Cable, alternate black
and white
675–650 B.C.

Typical Archaic Attic Designs (*contd.*)

1. PROTO-ATTIC: 710–610 B.C. (*contd.*)

Development of Animals

Fig. 90
Bird and plants
c. 705 B.C.

Fig. 91
Horse, plant and wavy
lines: note greater use
of curves than in
Geometric period –
compare with Figs. 24–26
c. 700 B.C.

Fig. 92
Lion: same comment
as above
700–675 B.C.

Fig. 93
Horses: same comment
as above
700–680 B.C.

Typical Archaic Attic Designs (*contd.*)

1. PROTO-ATTIC: 710–610 B.C. (*contd.*)

Development of Human Forms

Fig. 94
Early Proto-Attic
women: compare with
Fig. 23
c. 705 B.C.

Fig. 95
Charioteer: note
extensive use of wavy
lines
700–675 B.C.

Fig. 96
Odysseus, early mytho-
logical scene: note
greater use of curves in
man's body and absence
of wavy lines in
background
c. 650 B.C.

Typical Archaic Attic Designs (*contd.*)

2. ATTIC BLACK FIGURE TECHNIQUE: 610–480 B.C.

Human and Animal Figures

Fig. 97
600–575 B.C.

Fig. 98
580–575 B.C.

Fig. 99
570–565 B.C.

Fig. 100
550–540 B.C.

Typical Archaic Attic Designs (*contd.*)

2. ATTIC BLACK FIGURE TECHNIQUE: 610–480 B.C. (*contd.*)

Fig. 101
540–530 B.C.

Fig. 102
c. 530 B.C.

Fig. 103
Meander
c. 540 B.C.

Fig. 104
Palmette
c. 540–530 B.C.

Fig. 105
Linked lotus buds
and meander
c. 530 B.C.

Fig. 106
Ivy stem and leaves,
double spiral
c. 530 B.C.

Typical Archaic Attic Designs (*contd.*)

2. ATTIC BLACK FIGURE TECHNIQUE: 610–480 B.C. (*contd.*)

Fig. 107
c. 530 B.C.

Fig. 108
c. 520 B.C.

3. ATTIC BLACK FIGURE TECHNIQUE: WHITE GROUND: 530–480 B.C.

Fig. 109
c. 475 B.C.

Typical Archaic Attic Designs (*contd.*)

4. ATTIC RED FIGURE TECHNIQUE: 530–480 B.C.

Fig. 110
c. 525 B.C.

Fig. 111
510–500 B.C.

Fig. 112
c. 480 B.C.

Typical Archaic Attic Designs (*contd.*)

4. ATTIC RED FIGURE TECHNIQUE: 530–480 B.C. (*contd.*)

Red Figure Palmette

Fig. 113
c. 525–520 B.C.

Fig. 114
c. 525–520 B.C.

Fig. 115
c. 510–500 B.C.

Typical Archaic Attic Designs (*contd.*)

4. ATTIC RED FIGURE TECHNIQUE: 530–480 B.C. (*contd.*)

Red Figure Meanders

Fig. 116
500–490 B.C.

Fig. 117
500–490 B.C.

Other Red Figure Designs

Fig. 118
Base rays
530–520 B.C.

Fig. 119
Handle decoration
530–520 B.C.

Fig. 121
Tongues
c. 480 B.C.

Fig. 120
Chequer and tongues
530–520 B.C.

VII Classical Pottery (480–323 B.C.): Attic*

Attic Classical Red Figure pottery dominated the Greek world until about 323 B.C. Imitations were made chiefly in Boeotia, South Italy and Etruria.

CLASSICAL ATTIC RED FIGURE (c. 480–323 B.C.)
Background: Shiny black.
Colour of Designs: Orange-red and other colours were used in the latter part of the Classical period–including yellow-brown, yellow, white, red, purple, and even gold.
Decoration: As in the Late Archaic Red Figure, details were painted (not incised) in thin or wide lines; gradually the relief line was used less and less. Scenes were drawn primarily from life and were cheerful and gay. Painting became more important than the pot. Perspective appeared, particularly for chairs and tables. Humans were presented in three-quarters and full view (and less in profile). The profile eye replaced the Archaic full eye in profile faces. Emphasis was on anatomy, on humanism and on portrayal of effortless human dignity. Great attention was given to rounded forms and contours as well as to the fall, folds and shape of dress. Late in the Classical period, attempts were made to show figures in perspective so that they tended to leave the plane of the surface, sometimes even stepping out of the frame. Shading was also used. Scenes became crowded. Style and composition became clumsy, though individual figures on the fronts of pots were well executed, figures on the backs–usually a pair or trio of cloaked youths–became stereotyped and very poor. Men and women were painted in the same colour.
Repertory of Designs: Human figures dominated in scenes of daily life; gradually Dionysiac scenes became more frequent. Use of other ornamentation was restricted to lips, panel edgings, base, and round the handles of pots. These ornaments included primarily the lotus and the palmette (often very large and elaborate) and the simple meander. Towards the end of the period, there was greater use of hooks, stars, stripes and little animals on drapery, with garlands of leaves and berries intruding into the scenes. Gradually moulded relief tended to replace painting.
Shapes of Pots: At first shapes tended to become slimmer and the transition from one part to another to be less sharply defined than previously. Later, pots were less well made, swelling and emphasizing

* For greater detail on Attic and other Classical pottery, see Appendix 1, VII.

mouldings of foot and lip. In the 4th century, shapes became elongated. Generally pottery became practical and utilitarian.
Clay: Fine, red-orange.

CLASSICAL ATTIC WHITE GROUND (*c.* 480–*c.* 400 B.C.)

Background: White or whitish slip.

Colour of Designs: Matt (flat) black, red, purple, browny-red, yellow, rose, vermilion, sky blue, light purple. (Many of these colours were unstable and have washed off.)

Decoration: Decoration was in outline drawing–later supplemented by colour. The effect was softer than Red Figure, as the flush line of dilute paint gradually replaced the strong relief line even for outlines, and the flat washes of purple, browny-red and yellow used on drapery took over most of the design. Scenes tended to be melancholy, pathetic and tender, showing funeral scenes, farewells, a lady and maid, children, Charon and his boat, Hermes guiding the dead, Sleep and Death. Later, restrained scenes of mourning gave way to depictions of passionate grief. Lines became sketchy, green and mauve were added as colours.

Repertory of Designs: Generally the same as Red Figure, except that scenes were as described above. Men and women, often slender and fine-boned, were shown in pairs or threes.

Shapes of Pots: At first (480–450 B.C.), insides of cups, alabastra and pyxides were done in white ground. Later, however, the lekythos became the favourite pot for white ground work, being used for funeral dedications. As less use was expected, more perishable colours and a whiter, more friable slip could be used.

Clay: Fine, red-orange.

CLASSICAL ATTIC BLACK PAINTED (OR 'BLACK-GLAZED WARE') (480–323 B.C.)

Excellent Black Painted pottery (or as it is commonly miscalled, 'black-glazed ware') of the same type and quality as that produced in the Archaic period continued to be produced until about 400 B.C.; thereafter it declined in quality, but not in output. Because of its better clay and general quality plus tradition, Attic Black Painted pottery continued to be exported throughout the Classical period.

Occasionally this pottery had minor additions in colour–usually restricted to ovules on the deep lips of pelikai and hydriai. Also occasionally, in the late 5th and early 4th centuries B.C., a band of ornament, a wreath or festoon in white or yellow, appeared on hydriai.

Impressed decoration appeared about 460 B.C. on the inside of stemless cups. These were small and simple–a rosette of tongues surcharged with a star and enclosed in concentric circles, stamped palmettes, a chain of linked palmettes, ovules, or tongues.

Relief decoration of Classical pottery was rare.

Typical Classical Attic Designs

1. ATTIC RED FIGURE TECHNIQUE: 480–323 B.C.

Fig. 122
470–460 B.C.

Fig. 123
c. 450 B.C.

Fig. 124
435–430 B.C.

Typical Classical Attic Designs (*contd.*)

1. ATTIC RED FIGURE TECHNIQUE: 480–323 B.C. (*contd.*)

Red Figure Palmettes

Fig. 125
c. 480 B.C.

Fig. 126
c. 470–460 B.C.

Fig. 127
c. 460–450 B.C.

Red Figure Meanders

Fig. 128
480–470 B.C.

Fig. 129
c. 470 B.C.

Typical Classical Attic Designs (*contd.*)

1. ATTIC RED FIGURE TECHNIQUE: 480–323 B.C. (*contd.*)

Red Figure Meanders (*contd.*)

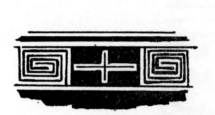

Fig. 130
460–450 B.C.

Fig. 131
c. 440 B.C.

Fig. 132
430–420 B.C.

2. ATTIC RED FIGURE TECHNIQUE: WHITE GROUND: 480–400 B.C.

Fig. 133
c. 445 B.C.

Fig. 134
c. 410–400 B.C.

VIII Hellenistic Pottery (323–146 B.C.)*

By 323 B.C., painted pottery as an art form was dead or at least dying. Painting was replaced by plastic designs in relief or impression, or by plain black or, later, plain red ware. Of the painted pottery, the two main types were *dark ground* (the so-called West Slope ware of the Eastern part of the Greek world, and Gnathian from Italy) and *light ground* (Lagynos ware from East of the Adriatic, Hadra ware from Alexandria, Canosa ware from Italy, and Centuripae ware from Sicily).

PAINTED HELLENISTIC POTTERY (*c.* 323–*c.* 146 B.C.)
Background: Dark or light (a white or yellowish slip).
Colour of Designs: White, yellow, gold and purple on the dark ground; black, brown, yellow-brown, yellow, pink, red, blue, etc., on the 'light ground'.
Decoration: Painted ornaments were simple and simply arranged—they were clearly 'painting on pottery' and not organically part of the pot. Plastic decoration, in relief or impression and modelled after metal-work, often covered most of the pot. The style required neither skill nor imagination.
Repertory of Designs: Wreaths, vines, festoons of ivy or laurel, abstract dolphins, round garlands, ribbons, musical instruments, necklaces, chequers, boxed and cross-hatched rectangles, opposed triangles, rosettes, sometimes human figures (usually women), and a few animals (winged or wingless horses and monsters).
Shapes of Pots: Shapes ranged from clumsy to elegant, with a tendency towards flowing curves and arbitrary angles and much imitation of metal-work.
Clay: Varied widely, but generally was coarser than in Red Figure pottery.

UNPAINTED HELLENISTIC POTTERY (*c.* 323–*c.* 146 B.C.)
1. *Hellenistic Black Painted (or 'Black-glazed Ware')*
     The plain black painted pottery which originated in the Archaic period reached its peak of excellence in the years *c.* 500–*c.* 400 B.C., but continued to be produced throughout the Hellenistic period, though it declined in quality. In degenerate form, it continued to be produced throughout the pre-Christian era. The black paint gradually became thinner and duller, and the Hellenistic ideal was a glassy, bluish, grey though the average product was often a muddy brown. Misfiring was frequent so that many pieces are

* For greater detail, see Appendix 1, VIII.

partly or wholly oxidized to red. Shapes tended to become clumsy and the repertory to decline to plates, saucers, bowls and dumpy jugs. Imitation of metal-work increased.

2. *'Pergamene' (or more generally 'Sigillata')*

In the Hellenistic period, pottery fired to a fine, even red became popular first in Greek Asia in about 150 B.C. Its production was continued after 146 B.C. throughout the Roman world for about two centuries and in the Eastern Empire until the 7th or 8th centuries A.D., when a true glaze was adopted generally. The repertory of shapes was, in general, limited to plates, saucers and open bowls.

The clay varied, but was generally fired to red or yellow. The true 'Pergamene' was a yellow clay and a glaze fired to a darkish, not very shiny red. Attic clay used in the Hellenistic period was browner and coarser than before. Arretine (Italian) clay was fired to a vivid red with a good sheen. Roman clay was pink and the paint was matt (dull) with a pink or brown tone.

DECORATION

1. *Painting in other colours* was very rare on Hellenistic Black Painted or Pergamene (Sigillata) ware.
2. *Impressed decoration* was relatively infrequent on Hellenistic Black Painted ware, consisting of careless rouletting and scattered palmettes (usually not linked and often without volutes at their base). On Pergamene and later Roman Sigillata, impressed decoration included fans, ferns, rosettes, little concentric circles, and potters' signatures.
3. *Relief decoration* (i.e. regular use of moulds to decorate and shape fine pottery) was an innovation of the Hellenistic period, when vase painting had decayed and pots were made in imitation of metal-ware. Among the Black Painted ware, the so-called 'Megarian bowls' (*c.* 300–*c.* 100 B.C.) are characteristic and the most widely known. They were roughly hemispherical bowls, entirely (except for the lip) decorated in relief with animals, human figures, abstract and vegetable designs more or less symmetrically arranged. Pergamene ware took over the technique, but did little with it. Later Sigillata, especially the Arretine, provide excellent examples of relief decoration.

Part 4

SHAPES AND USES OF GREEK POTTERY

Shapes and Uses of Greek Pottery

GENERAL

As noted in the Introduction, Greek pottery of the period 1050 to 323
B.C. reconciled to a unique degree the three demands of utility, of form
and of decoration. Part 3 dealt with decoration. Part 4 deals with uses
and forms.

To a large extent use determined general forms. Thus, utility dictated
the development of vessels for storage and shipment of wine, oil and
grain, as well as the provision of two vertical handles so that they could
be moved easily (*amphorae*). Another type of pot was designed to fetch
water from springs and fountains–it had two horizontal handles for
carrying and one vertical handle for dipping and pouring (the *hydria*).
As this pot was too large for convenient pouring by one person, a
pitcher (the *oinochoe*) was evolved for pouring small quantities of water
into a bowl (the *krater*) where the water was mixed with wine. Drinking
vessels appeared in a variety of forms. Other shapes (*lekythoi, aryballoi,
alabastra, askoi*) were created to contain toilet oils, perfumes and
condiments; and boxes (*pyxides*) were made for cosmetics and trinkets.

Each of these general forms experienced change in the seven hundred
or so years during which Greek pottery flourished as an art. For
example, the storage vessels (amphorae) varied in height from about
five feet to less than one foot. Smaller sizes of amphora were used as
decanters within the home, while other versions were used as grave-
markers. Different craftsmen also imposed their own variations. Styles
and fashions changed. This was true for all the general forms, though
the variations were of a lesser degree than for the amphorae.

Some centres of production tended to concentrate on certain forms.
For example, the potters of Corinth made a speciality of fine, thin-
walled, small forms such as pyxides, lekythoi, skyphoi and aryballoi.
And some forms, as has been mentioned in Part 3, were peculiar to, or
favoured by, certain schools of potters and painters: for example, the
fine 'Little Master' cups from Samos and the chalices from Chios.

Thus the forms themselves as well as the painting and the designs may
provide clues as to the age and origin of ancient Greek pottery.

The following section summarizes data on shapes and uses of the
general forms for the beginner. Appendix 2 provides additional details
as to variations within the general forms for those interested.*

* The data presented in this section on shapes of Greek pottery is drawn primarily
from R. M. Cook's *Greek Painted Pottery* and G. M. A. Richter's and M. J.
Milne's *Shapes and Names of Athenian Vases*.

MAJOR SHAPES OF GREEK POTTERY
WITH INDICATION OF USE

Greek pottery may be divided into eight general forms or major shapes based on use as follows:

English generic name or description of use	Name given to Greek forms Singular	Plural
1. Storage vessels for wine, oil and grain (though also used for other purposes)	Amphora	Amphorae
2. Pots for fetching and storing water	Hydria	Hydriai
3. Pitchers for pouring wine	Oinochoe	Oinochoai
4. Bowls for mixing wine	Krater	Kraters
5. Jugs and flasks for toilet oil, perfume, condiments, etc.*		
6. Boxes for cosmetics, trinkets, etc.	Pyxis	Pyxides
7. Cups for drinking wine†		
8. Plates and dishes for food‡		
9. Miscellaneous other forms		

The main forms and a few variations are described and shown below:

1. **Amphora:** A tall, two-handled pot with a neck narrower than the body: used for transportation and storage of wine, oil, grain, etc.; but smaller sizes sometimes used as decanters and larger sizes as grave-markers. Though some amphorae were several feet tall, the average was 30 to 45 cm. or 12 to 18 inches tall.
   There are two major sub-types:

Fig. 135

Fig. 136

a. Neck Amphora—neck is set off from the body

b. One-piece Amphora neck merges into body in one continuous curve

---

* Various names apply, including lekythos (lekythoi), araballos (araballoi). alabastron (alabastra), and askos (askoi).

2. **Hydria:** A pot with three handles, one vertical at the back and two horizontal at the sides: used for fetching water. The normal hydria was 30 to 45 cm. or 12 to 18 inches tall. Seen from the front, they might be mistaken for amphorae, but the two horizontal handles and the third vertical handle at the back serve as identification.

Fig. 137

3. **Oinochoe:** A pitcher with one handle placed vertically at the back: used for pouring wine. Early oinochoai compared in size with amphorae and hydriai, but can be mistaken for neither. The normal vessel was about 30 cm. or 12 inches tall. The profile might be mistaken for some lekythoi and aryballoi, but the latter are much smaller (ranging from 7½ to 20 cm. or 3 to 8 inches in height).

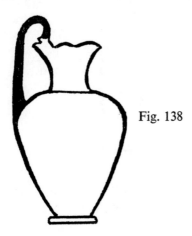

Fig. 138

† There are many names for drinking vessels used by the ancient Greeks and there is little agreement or consistency in their use. The more important include kotyle (kotylai), skyphos (skyphoi), and kylix (kylikes).
‡ There are also various names for plates and dishes.

4. **Krater:** A deep bowl with a wide mouth: used for mixing wine. The normal height was 30 to 45 cm. or 12 to 18 inches. The profile might be confused with that of the kotyle cup, but the latter is smaller, seldom exceeding 20 to 25 cm. or 8 to 10 inches in height.

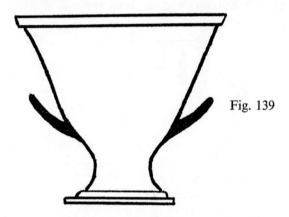

Fig. 139

5. **Flasks**

a. *Lekythos:* A small one-handled jug with a narrow neck and a deep mouth. It varied in height from 7½ to 30 cm. or 3 to 12 inches. As noted earlier, the profile of some types of lekythoi might be mistaken for certain oinochoai; the latter, however, are much larger.

   Some lekythoi have round bodies, some squat bodies. The classical shape is shown below.

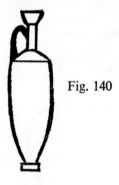

Fig. 140

b. *Aryballos:* An oil bottle with a narrow neck; and it may have two handles, one or none: used by athletes at the bath. The normal height is about 7½ cm. or 3 inches. The small size prevents confusion with other shapes.

Fig. 141

c. *Alabastron:* An elongated narrow-necked container for perfume; it had no handles, but sometimes it had string holes or ears. Normally these pots were 7½ to 20 cm. or 3 to 8 inches tall.

Fig. 142

d. *Askos:* A small flask wider than it was high, with a convex top and arched handle meeting the spout, which was at one side: used for oil.

Fig. 143

6. **Pyxis:** A round box for holding cosmetics and other toilet articles. Its height varied from about 5 to 18 cm. or about 2 to 7 inches.

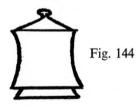

Fig. 144

7. **Cups**

Drinking vessels, as noted earlier, are called by many names and with little consistency. It appears that the word *kotyle* was a generic name for all cups; archaeologists, however, tend to reserve the name for the deep stemless cup with two horizontal handles. For simplicity and clarity's sake, typical examples shown below are restricted to the main types.

Fig. 145
a. SKYPHOS (or *Kotyle*)
A deep cup with no stem, and with two horizontal handles

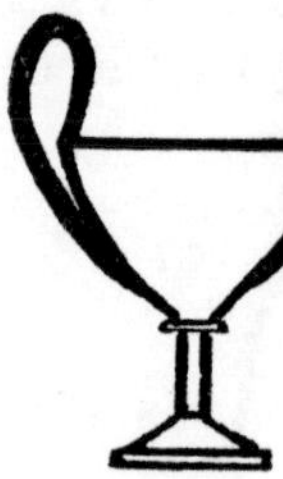

Fig. 146
b. KANTHAROS
A deep cup with or without
a stem, and with two
vertical handles

Fig. 147
c. KYATHOS
A deep cup with one
vertical handle

d. KYLIX (or *Cylix*)
A shallow cup with two
horizontal handles

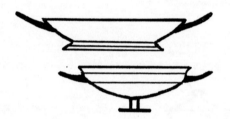

Fig. 148
1. Stemless Kylix

Fig. 149
2. Stemmed Kylix

8. **Plates, Dishes, etc.**
Plates and dishes varied widely in shape and size. An example of one
dish is given below.

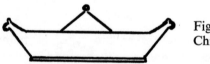

Fig. 150
Chiot dish

Appendix 1

PAINTING AND DESIGN
(ADDITIONAL INFORMATION)

I. Proto-Geometric and Geometric Pottery (900–c. 700 B.C.)

In addition to the Attic and Argive Geometric pottery outlined in the text as the two main centres, mention may be made of certain other centres as follows:

1. Corinthian Geometric: 900–725 B.C.

a. EARLY CORINTHIAN GEOMETRIC (900–800 B.C.)
Decoration: Usually confined to a single field, with the rest of the pot painted dark except for narrow groups of reserved bands.
Repertory of Designs: Sets of three or four horizontal zig-zags often connected to the frame by short strokes. The meander was rare.
Shapes of Pots: Trefoil-mouthed oinochoai and cups.

b. MIDDLE CORINTHIAN GEOMETRIC (800–750 B.C.)
Decoration: A little more complex, with normal main field stopped by narrow panels at each end and often underlined by a subsidiary horizontal strip.
Repertory of Designs: Hatched meanders, cross-hatched triangles, chevrons, zig-zags, wavy lines (upright or lying on side).

c. LATE CORINTHIAN GEOMETRIC (750–725 B.C.)
Background: Light.
Colour of Designs: Dark brown to red and white with a sheen.
Decoration: Sober and neat, but light in tone. Narrow stripes below the main panel alternating in paint and reserve.
Repertory of Designs: Opposed triangles, false spirals, intermittent groups of zig-zags or wavy lines spaced (sometimes alternately) in a narrow band around the pot.
Shapes of Pots: Oinochoai, kotylai, kraters, kantharoi, round pyxides and plates. Shapes were delicate and thin-walled.
Clay: Fine, lightish brown with a tendency towards pink or green.

2. Laconian Proto-Geometric and Geometric: 1000–650 B.C.

a. LACONIAN PROTO-GEOMETRIC
Background: Light (no slip).
Colour of Designs: Dark brown to blackish with metallic sheen.
Decoration and Designs: Cross-hatched triangles and narrow panels.
Shapes of Pots: Cups, oinochoai, small hydriai, usually with high conical feet and rims.

b. LACONIAN GEOMETRIC

Background: Light (sometimes slipped with grey, especially later).
Colour of Designs: Dark.
Decoration: Single band of continuous ornament with rest of pot painted dark.
Repertory of Designs: Concentric circles (often carelessly spaced and sometimes intersecting), triangles and lozenges (hatched or cross-hatched or even gridded). Later, step meanders, small solid meanders, occasional human figures, hatched birds, silhouette birds, quatrefoils and zig-zags, broken cables, rays and chequers.
Shapes of Pots: Cups, kraters, small bowls, low flat dishes, tall pyxides, oinochoai, lakaina.
Clay: Slipped-ware clay was coarse and pink, unslipped ware had finer clay.

3. **Boeotian Geometric:** 800–700 B.C.

Background: Light.
Colour of Designs: Dark (similar to Attic, but duller and less even).
Decoration: Usually drawing was clumsy and composition chaotic; the better pots, however, are difficult to distinguish from Attic.
Repertory of Designs: Human figures were attempted. Characteristic designs included: wavy lines of thin up-strokes and very thick down-strokes, spidery swastikas with more than four arms, rows of large concentric circles, alternating groups of upright straight and zig-zag lines, strips or narrow bands of zig-zags (vertical or horizontal)– sometimes joined to the frame by short strokes.
Shapes of Pots: Tall neck amphorae, large oinochoai, simple kantharoi or wide kotylai with high vertical handles.
Clay: Similar to Attic, but coarser and paler.

4. **Euboean Geometric:** 800–700 B.C.

Background: Light (slip sometimes used).
Colour of Designs: Dark.
Decoration and Designs: Small concentric circles on rims of cups, ring of dots round large circles, geometric ornaments often not hatched but drawn in outline and filled with cream slip or paint.
Shapes of Pots: Kotylai, cups.
Clay: Varies from Attic colour to a paler brown, usually fine, some·times chalky.

5. **Cycladic Proto-Geometric and Geometric:** 1000–700 B.C.

Origin: See Appendix 1, III.

a. CYCLADIC PROTO-GEOMETRIC (1000–900 B.C.)
Background: Light.
Colour of Designs: Dark.
Decoration and Designs: Modelled on Attic (and possibly on Argive) pottery. Local variations included: linking of grouped circles by bands of zig-zags or straight lines, and pendant concentric semi-circles.

b. CYCLADIC GEOMETRIC (900–700 B.C.)
Background: Light (slip sometimes used).
Colour of Designs: Dark.
Decoration and Designs: Differences between local and imported products were not uniform. The style was generally based on Attic Geometric, varied by clumsy incompetence and a few idiosyncrasies, especially in the use of small concentric circles on rims and other narrow zones, and a ring of dots round large circles. Late Cycladic Geometric pottery began to copy Corinthian styles with use of heavy vertical zig-zags and coarse striping on the lower parts of pots; later, Attic pottery became again the model.
Clay: Varies in texture and colour (see Appendix 1, III on clay of various centres).

6. **East Greek Proto-Geometric and Geometric:** 1000–650 B.C.

Origin: See Appendix 1, IV.

a. EAST GREEK PROTO-GEOMETRIC (1000–900 B.C.)
Background: Light.
Colour of Designs: Dark.
Decoration and Designs: Modelled on Attic (and possibly on Argive) pottery. Local variations included an excess of latticing and a linking of grouped circles by bands of zig-zags or straight lines.

b. EAST GREEK GEOMETRIC (900–650 B.C.)
Background: Light brown clay, occasionally (e.g. Samos and Chios) with a white slip.
Colour of Designs: Dark brown.
Decorations and Designs:
   Rhodes: Concentrated on upper part of the pots: at first one continuous band, later much division horizontally and vertically; little care for symmetry or balance. Designs included: irregular meanders

(hatched all in one direction), rows of large concentric circles and cross-hatched triangles and lozenges, opposed triangles (set vertically or in horizontal strips), alternate groups of oblique strokes, reserved triangles, rows of boxed chevrons and squares (later built into elaborate chessboard systems), square hooks (sometimes joined into a cross), birds with hatched bodies, and (often) plastic snakes.

Samos: Figures of animals and men and scenes of mourning were included in the decoration; the style was loose and unconsidered.

Chios: Also included some drawings of men and animals; meanders were sometimes filled with dots instead of hatching.

Common to all East Greek: Square hooks and meanders hatched in only one direction.

Shapes of Pots: Amphorae, trefoil-mouthed oinochoai, stemmed kraters, lekythoi, cups, kotylai, kantharoi.

Clay: See Appendix 1, IV on clay of various centres.

7. Cretan Proto-Geometric and Geometric

Peculiarities of Cretan pottery and lack of publications on its Proto-Geometric and Geometric periods render generalizations hazardous at present. (Those interested are referred to R. M. Cook, *Greek Painted Pottery*, pp. 12–13 and 33–34, and to the Collection in the Herakleion Museum.)

8. Italian-Greek Geometric

Etruria produced a true Geometric style clearly modelled on the Greek. Similarly, South West Italy, Apulia, Lucania and Sicily produced Geometric pottery modelled on the Greek. These schools have not been well studied. (See Cook, *op. cit.,* pp. 34–37.)

II Archaic Corinthian Pottery (725–550 B.C.)

Origin and Influence: The pottery of Corinth was widely exported to all parts of the Greek world, dominating the market until about 600 B.C. By 550 B.C., it had been replaced by Attic pottery. Corinthian pottery was widely imitated, especially in Etruria and South West Italy.

1. Early Proto-Corinthian: *c.* 725–700 B.C.

Background: Pale buff and pale green.

Colour of Designs: Black with other colours added for lesser features.

Decoration: Influenced by the East (the beginning of the 'orientalizing' animal style); at first animals and birds were rare. Decoration was often chaotic with Geometric patterns alongside the new black painted figure designs.

Repertory of Designs: Animals and birds, though initially rare, were capable of movement (not stiff, abstract, spiky Geometric silhouettes, but curved with eyes in white faces, and included cock, hen, etc.). *Plants* were usually symbolic, including hooked spirals, or coronas of leaf rays at shoulder or base, volutes, rosettes. *Other designs:* included cables and rings of solid triangles.

Shapes of Pots: Small, neat, precise, often round, including the aryballos and skyphos and to a lesser extent the oinochoe and straight-sided pyxis.

Clay: Fine whitish clay fired to pinkish tinge.

2. Middle Proto-Corinthian: *c.* 700–*c.* 650 B.C.

Colour of Designs: Black with greater use of purple, also brown, yellow and white for lesser features.

Decoration: Incised Black Figure technique with heavily engraved lines to show inner structure, and sometimes the outlines of figures: a style based on delicacy of line and balanced masses. Division between friezes composed of two or three narrow lines.

Repertory of Designs: Figures were drawn boldly with full rounded form and in vigorous tense positions. *Animals and birds:* Hittite lions and sphinxes (usually in facing pairs), dogs, hares, and birds (usually in files), horses, goats, centaurs. *Humans:* bearded men, gods and warriors, less frequent than animals. *Plants:* symbolic, spiral hooks, chains of lotus flowers and buds, palmettes, stalked dot rosettes, volutes, etc.

Shapes of Pots: Small, neat, miniature. The favourite shape was the aryballos, followed by the skyphos, flat-bottomed oinochoe, plain oinochoe and pyxis.

3. Late Proto-Corinthian, and Transitional:
c. 650–*c.* 640 B.C. and *c.* 640–*c.* 625 B.C. respectively

Colour of Designs: Same as earlier, but with more use of colour.
Decoration: Cheap, pretentious and mass-produced with a tendency to larger and more elongated animals, greater use of incision and colour for detail. Forms tended to be lumpy and postures wooden. Divisions between friezes were made of broad bands of dark paint with a few narrow stripes of purple, yellow or white (later).
Repertory of Designs: Animals and Birds: panther (full face and often in facing pairs replaced the lion), and a long frieze of three animals (i.e. a bull between a lion and a panther) became stereotypes. *Other designs:* filling ornament more dense, almost as important as animal figures, included stalked dot rosettes, tongues and scale designs.
Shapes of Pots: Tended to be larger, more pointed and elongated; included the pointed aryballos, alabastron, olpe, oinochoe, concave pyxis, etc.

4. Early Ripe Animal Style: *c.* 625–*c.* 600 B.C.

Decoration: Rich decoration, broad friezes, long careless animals, thick gaudy detail and filling ornament. The whole vase was treated as one panel for decoration.
Repertory of Designs: Animals and birds: the panther was the most common animal followed by the Assyrian lion with cross-hatched mane (replacing Hittite lion), boar, bull, goat, deer, hare, eagle, goose, owl, cock, and snake. Fantastic creatures also were common, including the siren, sphinx, griffin, griffin-bird, panther-bird, 'typhon' (or snake-tailed man), 'triton' (fish-tailed man), 'boread' (winged man), 'mistress of the beasts' (winged woman gripping a pair of animals), and gorgon. Wings appeared in a new fashion, one to front and one to back. Groups were usually heraldic (i.e. two facing animals with perhaps a third in the middle). *Plants:* lotus, palmette, in continuous chain or independently as doubled lotus, quadruple lotus or lotus-palmette cross, four lotus flowers or four lotus buds arranged radially and heavily cross-hatched. *Other designs:* solid incised rosette used heavily for filler.
Shapes of Pots: Tended to be larger: many round aryballoi and alabastra and the skyphos, olpe, oinochoe, concave pyxis, neck amphora and column krater.
Clay: Fine whitish clay fired to a greenish tinge.

5. **Middle Ripe Animal Style:** *c.* 600–*c.* 575 B.C.

Decoration: Style degenerated, figures became clumsy and dispirited.
Repertory of Designs: Smaller, filling ornament melted into rosettes
and little dots.

6. **Late Ripe Animal Style:** *c.* 575–550 B.C.

Background: Often the main fields were covered with a red slip containing red ochre to resemble Attic pottery.
Colour of Designs: Same, but more use of white and purple.
Decoration: Extinction of Animal Style.
Repertory of Designs: Shrunk down to sphinx, siren, panther, goat,
goose, griffin, griffin-bird and cock–all emaciated and drawn
perfunctorily.
Shapes of Pots: Most common included alabastron, skyphos,
aryballos, and the convex pyxis, plate, phiale, bowl, neck amphora
and column krater.

7. **Ripe Human Style:** *c.* 625–550 B.C.

Parallel with the Animal Style, there was also a Human Figure Style
in Corinth. It never, however, attained the rank of the Animal Style
and was inferior to the Attic Human Figure Styles. Figures included:
riders, soldiers, 'padded dancers'; sometimes battle scenes, horse
races, and scenes from life such as weddings, banquets, dances,
races. The figures were sometimes drawn in outline and sometimes
incised (often on the same vessel). Women were painted in white.

8. **Sub-Geometric Style:** *c.* 725–*c.* 600 B.C.

Corinthian Sub-Geometric pottery was similar to Geometric, but
enriched by spiral hooks, four-leaved rosettes, files of herons, snakes,
wavy lines with stars and swastikas in their curves, solid triangles
and solid rays (at first on shoulder, later around base).

9. **Linear Style:** *c.* 700–*c.* 600 B.C.

Made for common use: plain bands of paint, often with simple
designs–rays, hares, dogs running in silhouette, goats, soldiers, dots,
small chequers in bands.

10. **White Style:** *c.* 575–550 B.C.

Broad areas left blank and balance covered by simple bands or
meagre linear ornament.

III Archaic Cycladic Pottery 7th Century B.C.)

The Cyclades Islands include Thera, Rheneia, Delos, Melos, Tenos, Naxos, Paros, Siphnos, etc. Several styles of Early Archaic pottery of the Cyclades may be identified as follows:

1. **Theran Sub-Geometric:** *c.* 700 B.C.

   Origin: Thera.
   Background: Yellow slip.
   Colour of Designs: Dark.
   Decoration: The main decoration was placed on the front of the neck and on the shoulders in broad or narrow bands often complicated by panelling. The body was covered with sparse groups of stripes, loosely spaced and routine in precision. The general effect was arid and empty.
   Repertory of Designs: Hatched meanders, thick circles containing eight-leaved stars or four discs, quatrefoils, little birds, cross-hatched lozenges and triangles, thick horizontal zig-zags, false spirals (row of concentric circles joined by tangents), simple spirals and rows of dots; occasionally tongues and primitive floral chains appeared.
   Shapes of Pots: Most common was the large neck amphora; others included squat pithoi, kraters with low feet, plates, cups and oinochoai.
   Clay: Red, with volcanic impurities.

2. **'Wheel Group':** 7th Century

   Origin: Perhaps from Paros.
   Background: Reddish-brown (slip used rarely).
   Colour of Designs: Dark.
   Decoration: The shoulder was divided into two or three panels; the body was decorated with heavy lines or other simple patterns.
   Repertory of Designs: Heavy spoked circles on shoulder panels, zig-zags across corners of panels, dotted zig-zags, bands of short thick zig-zags, chains of lozenges, tall blobs and thick wavy lines.
   Shapes of Pots: Most common was the broad neck amphora.
   Clay: Reddish-brown and fine, but not uniform in colour or fineness.

3. **'Linear Island Group':** Late 8th to Early 7th Century

   Origin: Possibly from Thera, Delos or Paros.
   Background: Yellowish slip.

Colour of Designs: Dark brown.

Decoration: The principal field of decoration was the shoulder, which was divided into three panels; narrow stripes surrounded the neck, shoulder and foot with thin upright lines; the style was simple, but elegant, relying on lines.

Repertory of Designs: Vertical zig-zags, narrow stripes, heavy concentric circles (often flanked by four dots), quatrefoils, big lozenges that sprouted extra corners from sides, opposed or boxed triangles, rudimentary floral or curvilinear lines, various birds and lions. Animals were wiry and boneless, sometimes dotted, except on the shoulder. There was not much filling ornament.

Shapes of Pots: Neck amphorae, kraters and cups.

Clay: Reddish- to yellow-brown; fine; usually micaceous.

4. 'AD Group': Early 7th Century

Origin: Possibly from Rheneia, Siphnos, Kimolos or Paros.

Background: Creamy slip.

Colour of Designs: Dark and dull.

Decoration: The decoration was a crude contrast of dark and light: the whole surface covered with coarse, but effective, brushwork. The neck usually had an elongated horse covering the whole field. The shoulder usually had two or more animals grouped or in file. On the body were two to four bands of ornament with rays at the base.

Repertory of Designs: Horse (with or without wings, with a reserved head and with a dotted or chequered body), deer, griffin, lion (body elongated and exaggerated). Horizontal zig-zags and lozenges filled vacant spaces. Other designs included chequers, open cables, tall blobs, and short vertical zig-zags.

Shapes of Pots: Neck amphorae, hydriai, kraters, oinochoai and skyphoi.

Clay: Fine and brown.

5. 'Heraldic Group': Early 7th Century

Origin: Possibly from Thera, Siphnos, Naxos or Rheneia.

Background: Creamy slip.

Colour of Designs: Dark and shiny.

Decoration: The neck and shoulders (the main fields) were divided into main and subsidiary panels each having a pair of dancing animals or a single dancing animal. The lower half of the pot had sprawling designs. Drawing was cursory with more attention paid to general vertical effect than to accuracy of line or composition.

Repertory of Designs: Dancing lion or horse (winged or wingless),

head and neck of horse (always rubbery with reserved head and eyes), sphinx (with three-leaved drape over forelegs), floral designs, curvilinear lines, simple cables, latticing, lozenges (void or cross-hatched), S-shaped blobs, simple tongues and floral chains.
Shapes of Pots: The slim neck amphora was most common.
Clay: Reddish-brown.

6. **'Protome Group':** Mid 7th Century

Origin: To date, this group has been found only in the purification deposit on Rheneia; it may have come from Paros or Naxos.
Background: Cream slip.
Colour of Designs: Dark and dullish.
Decoration: A central panel and flanking panels on the neck and shoulder were characteristic. Deep bands on body and thick rays at the base were common. The style was one of sophisticated simplicity, balancing light and dark.
Repertory of Designs: Trio of S-blobs separated by grouped strokes on lip, head and neck of horse or forepart of lion on neck and shoulders (flanking panels had simple linear or floral designs); below the shoulder, appeared trios of S-blobs separated by grouped strokes, and bands of dark paint with two thin purple lines.
Shapes of Pots: Neck amphorae, hydriai, and cups.
Clay: Brown and micaceous.

7. **'Melian':** First Part of 7th Century

Origin: This group was first found on Melos, later on Delos, Rheneia, Siphnos, Paros, Naxos, Thasos, Icaria, Rhodes, at Kavalla, etc.
Background: Yellow slip.
Colour of Designs: Blackish-brown, purple, light brown: dull.
Decoration: The decoration was sluggish and monotonous covering the entire pot. On the neck there was usually a human or divine pair in the central panel with double volutes at the sides. On the body, in front, was a grand scene. On the back were unimportant figures. Below were bands of ornaments. On the foot were female heads or volutes with rays at the base. The decoration was unequal, coarse and angular.
Repertory of Designs: Human and divine pairs, double volutes, con-fronting animals (often horses), spirals, double spirals, female heads, reversed rays, mythological scenes, meanders, chevrons, tongues, lotus chains, large round dots, spiked dots, latticing, and eyes under handles.
Shapes of Pots: Large amphorae, kraters, hydriai, and plates.
Clay: Coarse brown, ranging to pink; slightly micaceous.

IV Archaic East Greek Pottery (700–500 B.C.)

East Greek pottery includes the products of the Greek cities of Asia Minor and the nearby islands (thus including, among others, the products of Old Smyrna, Lydian Sardis, Ephesus, Clazomenae, Aeolian Larisa, Miletus, Lesbos, Samos, Cos, Chios, Nisyros and Rhodes).

1. East Greek Bowls: 700–600 B.C.

Early Bowls: Inside painted dark, rim nicked, ring foot, painting on all of lower bowl.

Later Bowls: Inside painted with bands of white-red-white, rim smooth, foot moulded, rays around lower bowl.

Types: 'Bird bowls' (with hatched birds); 'rosette bowls' (with large dot rosettes); 'lotus bowls' (with lotus-flower decoration); and 'eye bowls' (with a large pair of eyes).

2. 'Wild Goat' Style: 650–500 B.C.

The most important of the East Greek styles is the 'Wild Goat' Style which is also known as Rhodian, Milesian and Camiran. The draughtsmanship of this style had a free, apparently spontaneous facility (actually it was too mass-produced to be spontaneous). The brushwork was thick and careless. Effect depended on mass and use of colour. It had a textile-like appearance. The wild goat was the characteristic item of design. Figures were reserved (i.e. painted in outline with white areas inside).

a. 'WILD GOAT' STYLE A (i.e. EARLY AND MIDDLE 'WILD GOAT') (650–600 B.C.)

Background: Yellow, cream or white slip.

Colour of Designs: Dark brown (sometimes fired to reddish), purple, white; no sheen.

Decoration: Emphasis of decoration was on the shoulder. Light filling ornament was well scattered. The style was highly decorative and gay. The dark lip often had eyes and rosettes in white. The neck was decorated with single cables, meanders or squares. Shoulders were the principal field for animals and geese. The belly had goats in friezes. The base had chains of lotus flowers and buds or long rays. Drawing was in outline technique.

Repertory of Designs: Animals: goats, spotted deer, lions, griffins– all common throughout the period; dogs and hares–early; boars and panthers rare; swallows *c.* 630 B.C. *Other Designs:* meanders, hook meanders, rosettes, cables, squares, rays, lotus (at first small and delicate, later large and bold) in chains, crosses, compact ornaments or even alone.

Shapes of Pots: Oinochoai, stemmed dishes, ringed foot dishes, kraters, dinoi (few amphorae or cups).

Clay: Coarse and gritty, usually fired from sandy-brown to pink, but sometimes chocolate to salmon red.

b. 'WILD GOAT' STYLE B (i.e. LATE 'WILD GOAT') (600–570 B.C.)
Background: A streaky whitish wash, sometimes omitted.
Colour of Designs: Dark brown (sometimes fired to reddish), with black, purple and white for details; little or no sheen.
Decoration:
(1) The Reserving Style continued in existence, but coarsened.
(2) A Black Figure technique with incision, based on uncritical acceptance and imitation of Corinthian Black Animal Figure appeared, but was coarse and blotchy. Animals were given the place of honour on the neck.
Repertory of Designs:
(1) Reserving Style: stubby goats, angular sphinxes, dogs, bulls, boars, griffins, lumpy lotus, long bunches of leaves, solid filling ornaments, heavy dividing bands.
(2) Black Figure Animal Style: lions, boars, bulls, goats, sphinxes, griffins, geese (or swans).
Shapes of Pots: The long, narrow, high-necked oinochoe, the amphora, krater, stemmed dish, ringed foot dish and plate.
Clay: Coarse, gritty, usually fired from sandy-brown to pink, but sometimes chocolate to salmon-red.

3. Grey Ware (or Bucchero)

A special type of unpainted grey pottery with decorations made of ridges and impressed or incised patterns (including hatched meanders and triangles), appeared first in the Geometric period and continued into the Archaic period, but only in Aeolis.

4. Chiot Styles: 700–550 B.C.

Background: Hard white slip.
Colour of Designs: Dark brown with olive tinge, golden-brown, buff, with purple or white for details.
Decoration:
a. 'Wild Goat' Style: differentiated by horseshoe roundels, pendant

triangles, dots on bellies of animals and on volutes, scattering of ornaments on animals.

b. Black Figure Animal Style: a careless, small-scale adaptation of the Middle Ripe Corinthian with rows of crouching sphinxes or frilled lions, bulls, drunken male dancers with protruding rumps, sirens; filling ornament of Corinthian rosettes and half rosettes.

c. Chiot Chalice Style (600–550 B.C.): included both human and animal figures (not together), sphinxes (seated or standing), lions, no filling ornaments; single animal figure on each side of chalice, or human scenes (battles, parties, races, mythological scenes, etc.). Inside of chalice first slipped, then covered with dark paint, then ornamented in white and purple; cross or rosette in centre with lotus flowers round the edge.

Shapes of Pots: Chalice and phiale, very thin.

Clay: Sandy, fired from lightish- to reddish-brown.

5. **Ionian Little Master Cups:** *c.* 550 B.C. (probably from Samos)

Background: Red clay.

Colour of Designs: Black.

Decoration: Decoration was free, loose and careless, but well selected and original. Both sides of the lip of the cups were reserved: outside decorated with doubled myrtle or ivy leaves, inside with the same or with birds and animals. Fauna were shown in black silhouette. Details were either incised or so finely reserved as to be equal to incision.

Shapes of Pots: Similar to Siana and Lip cups.

Clay: Reddish-orange, similar to Attic clay.

6. **Fikellura:** 575–500 B.C. (Southern part of East Greek region—probably Rhodes and Samos)

Background: Creamy yellow to white slip.

Colour of Designs: Dark brown to red (purple used only on early pieces, white used rarely—for eyes, etc.).

Decoration: Based on 'Wild Goat' and careless, but original. Lip decorated with rough vertical strokes; the neck with double cable, meander, or square and meander cross; the three-reeded handle with coarse blobs; the body with a variety of decoration in a free field. Filling ornament was light. There was no difference in colour for men and women.

Repertory of Designs: Animals and birds: in full silhouette with details reserved: lion, panther, bull, boar, deer, goat, sphinx, griffin, dogs chasing hares, ducks and partridges in file—repertory gradually

reduced to dogs, hares and birds. *Humans:* at first neat and small, later larger and clumsy: scenes include drunken revels, pygmies fighting cranes, humorous scenes, sometimes single figures, fanciful figures (winged man, hare-headed man, winged dog-headed man, etc.). *Other designs:* crescents, vertical strokes, single and double cables, meanders, square and meander crosses, volutes, spirals, net patterns (often dotted), scale patterns, lotus, chains of lotus buds, ivy or doubled myrtle leaves, enclosed palmettes, leaf rosettes.
Shapes of Pots: The squat amphora was characteristic, also oinochoe and small cup.
Clay: Gritty, buff to pink.

7. **Clazomenian:** 550–525 B.C. (Northern part of East Greek region – Clazomenae)

Background: Light clay.
Colour of Designs: Black with fine sheen, purple and white for details.
Decoration: Done in Black Figure technique, the style was decorative, but there was no interest in anatomy or composition. Human figures occupied the principal fields; animals occupied the secondary fields; floral and abstract designs occupied the less important areas. Incision was careless. White colour was used for both males and females.
Repertory of Designs: Human: women holding hands in file, satyrs, revellers, processions, riders, chariots, mythological scenes. *Animal:* sketchy, long-necked birds in file are characteristic. *Other:* black scales with large white drop or white scales with purple drop, crescents on a dark band, large palmettes with matted incised fringes, palmette crosses, small stars, rows of dots between pair of incised lines.
Shapes of Pots: The neck amphora, hydria, very large low pyxis, krater.
Clay: Leathery brown (lighter than Attic).

8. **Vroulian Cups:** 600–525 B.C. (Rhodes)

Background: Near black and shiny.
Colour of Designs: Light colours with purple.
Decoration: The whole cup was painted black except (sometimes) for a reserved band at handle level. Ornamentation was large, boldly incised and emphasized with purple.
Repertory of Designs: Palmettes, enclosed palmettes, lotus flowers and buds, rosettes, zig-zags, opposed triangles.

Shapes of Pots: Thin-walled cups with low off-set rims.
Clay: Fine, yellowish- to reddish-brown.

9. Banded Ware

Cheap, for common use, decorated simply with bands of paint; clay coarse, fired from pink to pale brown, very rarely slipped; some of shiny orange-brown clay with good near-black paint.

V Archaic Attic Pottery (700–480 B.C.)

During the early part of the 6th century, Attica regained from Corinth its position as the dominant centre for production of Greek painted pottery; by the year 550 B.C., this dominance was complete, and remained unchallenged until the decline of pottery as an art form. The stages of this rebirth may be traced as follows:

1. **Proto-Attic:** 700–610 B.C.

   Proto-Attic pottery, which is coarser, less well disciplined and made of less fine clay than Attic Geometric pottery, may be divided into three distinct stages as follows:

a. EARLY PROTO-ATTIC (*c.* 710–*c.* 680 B.C.)
Background: Light, yellowish slip frequent.
Colour of Designs: Dark, uneven, dull with white and yellowish-white for details.
Decoration: In Early Proto-Attic pottery, there was a mixture of the older Geometric with the new Orientalizing Style of animals and flowing lines plus native Attic development of Geometric designs and figures. Style was crude and massive. Balancing of groups was not always symmetrical. The technique was outline drawing in dark paint with major portions of figures in silhouette and occasional poor incision.
Repertory of Designs: New (non-Geometric) designs included: lions, horses, dogs, cocks, eagles, crick-necked birds, men and women (more curved and more natural in pose than Geometric), sphinx, and centaur, all with eyes. Floral and other designs included: solid rays, double spirals, lozenges with spiral hooks, spotted leaves, palmettes, heart-shaped pairs of spirals, hooks and heavy use of horizontal zig-zags.
Shapes of Pots: There was a continual trend towards slimmer pots with slurred angles. Shapes included the hydria (new), amphora and krater in particular, and globular oinochoe, stemmed bowl, mug, skyphos, and round aryballos.
Clay: Pale, coarse.

b. BLACK AND WHITE STYLE (*c.* 680–*c.* 650 B.C.)
Background: Light, yellowish slip common.
Colour of Designs: Dark, with generous use of white.
Decoration: In contrast to the earlier Proto-Attic, where the sil-

houette was strong, the Black and White Style used light and dark almost equally in outline drawing. The result was a style of broad contrasts. Planning, however, was poor so that figures were unequal, and composition was often lop-sided. Both white lines and incision were common for details. Filling detail became more sparse.

Repertory of Designs: Solid figures of humans and animals, large almond-shaped eyes and heavy brows, figures were ill-proportioned (light and dark were not indicative of sex). Other designs included: spiral hooks with bird beaks, repeated palmettes (reproduced until they looked like bunches of grapes), solid rays, cables, rosettes and rows of leaves–often painted alternately in black and white.

Shapes of Pots: Tall krater and kotyle krater.

Clay: Pale, coarse.

c. LATE PROTO-ATTIC (*c.* 650–*c.* 610 B.C.)

Background: Light, yellowish slip common.

Colour of Designs:

(1) Briefly purple was used so liberally that a three-colour school developed with liberal use of white for details.

(2) Later, white lost ground so that only black and purple were used.

(3) Briefly also, there was a polychrome style employing reds, yellow, browns, and bluish-green.

Decoration: During this period, animals were painted in Black Figure technique (solid silhouette with details incised or painted with purple or white), while human figures continued to be done in the old outline technique. Scenes were clearly mythological. Painting was planned carefully and well executed. Filling ornament became light and subdued.

Repertory of Designs: Animals and humans, gorgons, and birds constituted the main designs. Other designs included: floral chains, mill-sail patterns, oblique meanders, neat dot rosettes and incised rosettes.

Shapes of Pots: Large amphora, kotyle krater (often with a lid and a stand), one-piece amphora; coils of clay were common on handles.

Clay: Pale and coarse.

2. **Black Figure:** 610–450 B.C.*

Black Figure Attic pottery gradually (by 550 B.C.) came to dominate over all other Greek pottery. Its development passed through three fairly distinct phases before it was replaced by the Red Figure

---

* Though the Archaic period is considered to end with the year 480 B.C., when Athens was sacked by the Persians, it is more convenient to follow the Black Figure technique to its end in about 450 B.C.

technique; one special type, the Panathenaic amphora, continued in use alongside the Red Figure for many years.

a. CORINTHIAN-INFLUENCED BLACK FIGURE (*c.* 610–*c.* 550 B.C.)
Background: Orange-red.
Colour of Designs: Shiny black, purple and some white.
Decoration: The whole surface of the pot was no longer regarded as a single field for decoration. Instead, definite bands and panels were created on the neck, shoulder and body. Style became 'narrative' in its presentation of mythological scenes and meticulous in its precision and use of titles to identify the participants. Potmakers' and painters' names appeared for the first time on pots. After the 570's, it became conventional to paint men in black (at first with purple faces) and women in white. The face was almost always in profile, but with an almond-shaped frontal eye; chest and upper body was in frontal view and from waist down in profile. Incision became increasingly more important for details, with purple or white used for larger effects painted over the black of the main figure. Animals, unless included in the main narrative scenes, were relegated to rims or lower parts of pots and were arranged in perfunctory rows and tiers.
Repertory of Designs: Small figures in numerous strip panels showing gods, heroes, and men in mythological scenes involving battles, ships, chariots, etc., mythological creatures such as gorgons, harpies, boreads, satyrs, lapiths, centaurs, pygmies, 'mistress of the beasts', sphinx, and griffin, as well as normal animals such as horses, boars, lions, panthers, dogs and hares. Floral and other designs included: lotus buds and flowers, palmettes, bands of dots, chequers, tongues and rays.
Painters and Potters: For the first time painters and potters can be recognized either by their styles or by actual signatures. Among the most famous of this period were: the Nettos Painter, the Gorgon Painter and Sophilos.
Shapes of Pots: In general, small fine shapes like the cup, the krater and the dinos were the favourites for painters, although neck amphorae, one-piece amphorae, kotyle kraters, bowls, kantharoi, skyphoi, olpes, lekanides, column kraters, hydriai, lekythoi, plates, alabastra, aryballoi and pyxides were also common. Special mention may be made of cups and two types of amphorae:
(1) Stemmed cups appeared in the 580's and were popular thereafter.
    (a) Comast Cup: 585–570 B.C.; low flaring foot, no stem, wide shallow bowl and short offset lip, looks a bit top-heavy. Decorated usually with three designs on each side, floral designs under the handle and plain black inside.*

* See Fig. A–119.

(b) Siana Cup: 575–550 B.C.; flaring foot, very short thick stem, wider, but shallow bowl, definite lip with a high rim. Decoration was balanced in light and dark, the lower part of the bowl and foot was usually black, but sometimes was elaborately patterned. The main decoration usually extended over the bowl and lip; sometimes the lip had one frieze and upper bowl another.*

(2) Tyrrhenian Amphorae: 575–550 B.C.; squat neck, long egg-shaped body and spreading foot; painted in rough careless style, generally pretentious and inferior, inscriptions generally were nonsense or blobs made to imitate letters.

(3) The Panel Amphora (a solid one-piece amphora): 575–550 B.C.; with a reserved window showing a human or animal head.

Clay: Fine orange-red.

b. MATURE BLACK FIGURE (*c. 570–c. 525 B.C.*)

Background: Orange-red.

Colour of Designs: Shiny black, purple and white (white usually only for skin of women).

Decoration: Decoration concentrated on a single large field formed by bands of decoration. A picture of a single incident with five or six figures replaced the narrative strip which had many figures. Figures were drawn larger and anatomy became more coherent with more natural poses and attention being given to drapery and folds of clothing. Depiction of 'mood' became important–usually dignified, sombre, pathetic, severe or grim. Scenes usually depicted the moment of crisis in a story. Subsidiary ornament lost its importance: narrow bands of lotus and palmettes framed the central panel; rays banded the base; chains of lotus or other ornaments were used sparingly.

Repertory of Designs: Large figures in one panel: gods, heroes and men in mythological scenes, animals as needed in the scenes, satyrs, maenads, dolphins, etc. Subsidiary ornament included: narrow bands of lotus flowers and buds, and palmettes, narrow rays, simple meanders, volutes, ivy leaves; the ornamentation was usually careless.

Painters and Potters: Kleitias, Ergotimos, Nearchos, Tleson, Exekias, the Amasis Painter, Sakonides, the Phrynos Painter, the Painter of Acropolis 606, and Lydos.

Shapes of Pots: In general the favourite shapes were: the one-piece amphora, neck amphora and cups. The hydria, olpe, oinochoe, lekythos, and column krater came second. Moulding was precise and delicate.

* See Fig. A–120.

Cups of particular note include the following (all evolved from the Siana cups):

(1) Lip Cup: 565–535 B.C.; definite flat foot, tall thin stem meeting a wide shallow bowl very sharply, a very definite slightly out-curving lip set off sharply from the bowl. The outside of the lip, the handle frieze, the narrow strip on the lower part of the bowl, the sharp edge and underside of the foot, the hollow of the stem and the inner face of the handles were all reserved (i.e. unpainted), the rest black. The lip and upper bowl were divided by a black line and were the areas used for painted scenes; decoration was usually on the lip, while the upper bowl had an inscription or was left blank. The inside of the bowl was black with small reserved circles in the centre.*

(2) Band Cup: 550–520 B.C.; definite flat foot, taller and slimmer stem meeting a wide deep bowl at a sharp angle–often, however, masked by a fillet; the black concave lip passed into the bowl in a smooth curve. Decorative accent was on the handle frieze; the lip, lower bowl and stem were painted black.†

(3) Droop Cup: 560–510 B.C.; characterized by the broad unpainted channelling of the top of the stem, the convex edge of the foot, a black border on the inside of the stem, decoration on the lower bowl with a chain of buds separating lower bowl from handle frieze, decoration of the handle frieze with upside-down sil-houette animals and rays on the base.‡

(4) Eye Cup: 540–500 B.C.; definite foot, broad stumpy black stem, surmounted by a purple fillet, low rounded single-curved bowl with a small lip and black upcurving handles. The main feature was a pair of large eyes on the exterior of the bowl.§

Clay: Fine, orange-red.

c. LATE BLACK FIGURE (*c.* 530–*c.* 450 B.C.)

Background: Orange-red.

Colour of Designs: Shiny black and purple (with use of purple tending to decrease, however).

Decoration: In the Late Black Figure period, artists were influenced by the Red Figure technique which had developed in about 530 B.C. Pots were sometimes done in Black Figure on one side and Red Figure on the other, but even if they were not, Red Figure techniques were attempted in the Black Figure designs. Composition became fuller, with closer grouping of figures and much foliage. All the

* See Fig. A–121.
† See Fig. A–122.
‡ The profile of the droop cups is similar to the 'Little Master' cups of Fig. A–121.
§ See Figs. A–127 to A–129.

figures 'acted' conveying mood by facial expressions, movement of hands, and attitudes. Composition and detail, however, tended to become fussy, finicky and tiresome. Scenes tended to show everyday life (sometimes with charm and humour) rather than heroic grandeur.

Repertory of Designs: Same as in earlier Black Figure work except that the soft chiton replaced the heavy peplos as styles of dress changed.

Painters and Potters: The Lysippides Painter, Psiax, and the Antimenes Painter.

Shapes of Pots: Most common were the neck amphora, hydria, one-piece amphora, lekythos, cup and Nikosthenic amphora. Others included the column krater, plate, alabastron, oinochoe, stamnos and pelike; the eye cup remained common.

*Panathenaic Amphorae:** c. 566 B.C. to 3rd century A.D.; these deserve a special mention. Always done in the Black Figure technique, even after this technique had become an anachronism, these amphorae were given as prizes (filled with oil) at the Panathenaic Games (inaugurated c. 566 B.C.). They bear the official inscription 'From the Games at Athens' and an armed Athena on the main panel of the amphora. In about 530 B.C., columns were added on each side of Athena with a cock on top of one. A chain of lotus and palmettes on the neck with tongues below are characteristic. On early Panathenaic amphorae, Athena faced to the left. Sometime between 359 and 348 B.C., she was made to face to the right, a position retained thereafter. On the back of the amphorae were pictures of the events. Orders for these amphorae were placed with the best artists of the time including Lydos, the Kleophrades Painter, the Berlin Painter and the Achilles Painter. During most of the 4th century B.C. it was the practice to add the name of the archon (chief magistrate) to the vase. The earliest name is that of Hippodamos (375–374 B.C.): the last is Polemon (312–311 B.C.).

Clay: Fine, red-orange.

3. Red Figure: 530–480 B.C.

Development of the Red Figure technique by the painters of Athens in about 530 B.C. was a revolutionary change in the decoration of pottery. It was not a simple reversal of colours from the Black Figure technique. The Black Figure technique is an engraver's technique; the Red Figure is a draughtsman's technique. The optical balance of dark and light also is totally different. The Red Figure technique permitted a rounder illusion of humanity; the human figure became

* See Fig. A–21.

9

a study in itself (not as a component of a scene), a figure with muscles, individuality and moods.

In this technique the figure was drawn in outline on a light ground; inner detail was drawn with a brush (not incised). Two kinds of lines were used: (1) a flat line, often diluted so as to fire as a light brown, and (2) the 'relief line', a fine ridge of shiny black paint that can be seen and felt as a ridge used to emphasize major details. Once the figure was outlined and details drawn, the background was filled in with a heavy solution that fired black.

a. EARLY ARCHAIC RED FIGURE (*c.* 530–*c.* 500 B.C.)
Background: Shiny black.
Colours of Designs: Orange-red; purple was used for beards and hair.
Decoration: Initially, the Red Figure technique was merely a rendering of the Black Figure in another colour, remaining stiff, and for a while the incision of details continued (incision for outline of hair was common). The eye continued full though in a profile face, while the pupil was set further forward. Freedom of pose and suppleness gradually increased. Figures continued to remain in the plane of the surface of the pot despite attempts at foreshortening. As the light short-sleeved chiton replaced the heavy sleeveless peplos, greater attention was given to drapes and folds.
Repertory of Designs: Mythological scenes and battles remained common, but scenes of human life grew more important. Ornaments used for framing remained much the same as in the Black Figure technique – single and double chains of lotus and palmettes. The palmette, however, was often large enough to be drawn in outline.
Shapes of Pots: Simple, rhythmically designed, and finely executed, rounded rather than angular, including in the first place the one-curve cup, followed by the one-piece amphora, pelike, squat-necked stamnos and rounded hydria.
Potters and Painters: The Andokides Painter, Euphronios, Euthymides, Epiktetus, Psiax, Oltos, Skythes.
Clay: Orange-red and fine.

b. LATE ARCHAIC RED FIGURE (*c.* 500–*c.* 480 B.C.)
Background: Shiny black.
Colour of Designs: Orange-red; purple was used rarely.
Decoration: Where Early Red Figure painters aimed at strength, the later Archaic painters aimed at grace. The three-quarters view of the torso became common. The profile eye began to replace the full eye. The hair outline was reserved instead of incised. Groupings became less formal. Dress was drawn to conform to the body inside.
Repertory of Designs: Scenes of human life replaced the mythological

scenes even more. Ornaments included the simple meander (often interrupted by squares containing crosses) and palmette; ornamentation was relatively sparse.

Shapes of Pots: The one-curve cup remained the most popular; others included the neck amphora, pelike, stamnos, rounded hydria, krater, lekythos and alabastron.

Potters and Painters: Epiktetus, the Kleophrades Painter, the Berlin Painter, Myson, the Panaitios Painter, the Brygos Painter, Douris, and Makron.

Clay: Orange-red and fine.

VI Other Schools of Archaic Pottery (700–480 B.C.)

In addition to the main schools of Archaic Greek pottery outlined in the text (Corinthian, Attic, Laconian, Cycladic and East Greek), mention should be made of certain other schools as follows:

1. Boeotia

a. SUB-GEOMETRIC OR ORIENTALIZING STYLE (700–600 B.C.)
Background: Light; creamy slip or wash.
Colour of Designs: Dark, uneven and dull.
Decoration: Decoration was a mixture of Geometric and Orientalizing figures.
Repertory of Designs: Primitive floral designs, vertical zig-zags in groups, simple banding.
Shapes of Pots: Large amphorae (with high conical foot and short neck), other amphorae, plus miscellaneous other pots.
Clay: Coarse fired buff to pink.

b. BIRD CUP GROUP (560–480 B.C.)
Background: Light; at first cream, later white slip; surface powdery.
Colour of Designs: At first dark with red and purple; later purple and yellow used more.
Decoration: Ornamentation was upside down.
Repertory of Designs: Upside-down birds, palmettes and cross-hatched triangles, zig-zags and bands.
Shapes of Pots: Cups and kantharoi.
Clay: Buff or pink.

c. BOEOTIAN BLACK FIGURE (early 6th century to 480 B.C.)
Background: Light; light brown–sometimes with a reddish wash.
Colour of Designs: Dark; dull and streaky.
Decoration: Animal Style was common, but animals were surrounded with thick filling ornament; human figures were rare. Some figures were in full silhouette; incision and added colour were often not employed.
Repertory of Designs: Black Figure animals (tame and thin), human figures rare, figures surrounded with thick filling ornament–floral designs at first (later these disappeared).
Shapes of Pots: Kantharos, tripod pyxis, lekane, skyphos, and cup.
Clay: Pale brown.

2. Euboea

EUBOEAN (700–480 B.C.)
Background: Light.
Colour of Designs: Dark, similar to Attic with use of purple and white.
Decoration: Main decoration panel was between the handles. Much of pot was covered simply with dark paint. Early figures were drawn in partial outline with white (no incision) for details. Later incision was used. Style was uncouth.
Repertory of Designs: Large and small vertical zig-zags in a close row or spaced in groups, upright bars shaped like a sausage, animals, humans and monsters (alone in main panel).
Shapes of Pots: Amphorae were favoured.
Clay: Similar to Attic.

3. Italy

Greek colonies in Italy (Southwest Italy, Sicily, Apulia, Lucania, etc.) imported and produced Greek pottery. Corinth, and later Athens, dominated the Italian market and their wares influenced local production. Greek vase-makers and painters also emigrated to Etruria where they influenced the native products. Among the more important Archaic Greek types of pottery produced in Italy, the following are worthy of note.

a. ITALO-CORINTHIAN (700–550 B.C.) (Etruscan imitation of Corinthian)
Background: Light, sometimes with a cream slip.
Colour of Designs: Dark; dull and thin; free use of purple and white.
Decoration: Based on Corinthian Animal Style, but less sensitive to logical rules and conventions, figures were grotesquely proportioned and shoulder markings converted into meaningless rings.
Repertory of Designs: Animals: lions, deer, three-winged creatures, balloon-bodied birds. *Other designs:* overlapping semi-circles, 'Phoenician palmettes', simple bands, tongues, Laconian dots and squares, opposed triangles, dots.
Shapes of Pots: Varied: olpe, oinochoe, plate, cup, aryballos, alabastron, etc.–often embellished with bolster around neck and channels or ridges on body.
Clay: Fine to coarse, light cream to dull medium brown; coarse ware fired to pink.

b. ETRUSCAN BUCCHERO (or Grey Ware) (675–540 B.C.)
Background: Shiny black (best), light and yellowish-grey (poorer).

Colour of Designs: Usually not coloured (white, red, purple and blue occasionally used).

Decoration: Decoration was boldly incised or pricked. Generally decoration was subordinate to shape.

Repertory of Designs: Double spirals, hatched or boxed rays, vertical striations, horizontal zig-zags, rosettes, fans (open or closed), birds and even horses. (Sometimes the incision was filled with white or red paint.) Late Bucchero had thick tongues, moulded animals, stamped figures and ornaments.

Shapes of Pots: Varied: amphora, oinochoe, olpe, cup, kantharos, kyathos, chalice, etc. – often with plastic moulded shapes.

Clay: Fine, reduced in firing to grey (or poorer, to a brown or pale grey).

c. ETRUSCAN BLACK FIGURE (550–480 B.C.) (Etruscan imitation of Attic)

Background: Light, sometimes slipped with yellowish- or reddish-brown.

Colour of Designs: Dark and dull, brownish-black, purple and white for details; some sheen.

Decoration: Decoration was careless and showed lack of comprehension of Attic models. Groups were made up of stock figures often in meaningless relations. Principal field of decoration was on the shoulder; other fields were: two on the belly and one on the neck. Drawing of outline and detail was weak, relying on diffusion and much use of purple and white.

Repertory of Designs: Long rays on base, single or double band of meanders and stars, net pattern, partridges, sea-horses, tritons, panthers (with blank white eyes), multi-coloured animals, women with painted coifs, boots with upturned toes, lanky birds, ivy leaves.

Shapes of Pots: Varied: neck amphora, one-piece amphora, oinochoe, chalice, hydria, etc.; pots were badly proportioned.

Clay: Muddy, not too well refined; dirty yellow to pink.

d. CHALCIDIAN (560–520 B.C.) (Probably made by settlers from Euboea in South Italy)

Background: Orange.

Colour of Designs: Shiny, near black; golden brown with added purple and white.

Decoration: Done in Attic Black Figure Style, the painting was broad and robust with rounded figures. Design continued under the handles. There was little inner detail or overlapping. Scenes included mythology and human life.

Repertory of Designs: Frontal four-horse chariot was typical; also lions or panthers mauling a deer; humans had weak profiles with receding foreheads and long skulls; female eyes were often purple; drapes revealed back contours on figures. Squares of interlaced lotus or ivy were characteristic; palmettes, lotus flowers and bud chains were common.

Shapes of Pots: Varied: large and small neck amphora, one-piece amphora, hydria, column krater, cup, oinochoe, skyphos, pyxis, etc.; finely modelled; handles were high, extending above the pot rim.

e. CAERETAN (550–500 B.C.) (Thought to have been made by one or two East Greek masters who fled to Italy to escape the Persians)
Background: Light to orange.
Colour of Designs: Shiny and dark with purple, white and buff.
Decoration: Decoration was in Black Figure Style with incised lines. Emphasis was on the belly, with a large field in front and two shorter fields behind on either side of the vertical handle. Heracles was a favourite item. Figures were full, rounded, fleshy and solid–motion appears jerky.
Repertory of Designs: Mythological scenes, hunts, battles, etc., floral designs.
Shapes of Pots: All were hydriai.
Clay: Light yellowish-brown, warm brown, orange-red.

Archaic Designs

1. BOEOTIAN STYLES: 600–480 B.C.

Fig. A-1
Typical Boeotian
upside-down
bird
c. 550 B.C.

Figs. A-2 and A-3
Rosette and lattice
c. 550 B.C.

Fig. A-4
Palmette
c. 550 B.C.

Archaic Designs (*contd.*)

2. CHALCIDIAN STYLES: 560–520 B.C.

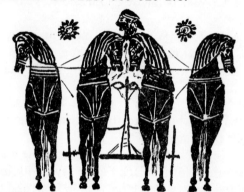

Fig. A-5
Typical Chalcidian
horses
c. 540 B.C.

Fig. A-6
Typical warrior's
shield
540–530 B.C.

Fig. A-7
Alternating lotus
flowers and palmettes
540–530 B.C.

Fig. A-8
Linked lotus buds
540–530 B.C.

3. CAERETAN STYLES: 550–500 B.C.

Fig. A-9
Typical Caeretan hare
540–530 B.C.

Archaic Designs (*contd.*)

3. CAERETAN STYLES: 550–500 B.C. (*contd.*)

Fig. A-10
Ivy leaves and berries
540–530 B.C.

Fig. A-11
Caeretan human
540–530 B.C.

VII Classical Pottery (Red Figure)
(*c.* 480–*c.* 323 B.C.)

Attic Red Figure pottery was exported throughout the Greek world, completely dominating the market during most of the 5th century B.C. Imitators in Boeotia, South Italy and Etruria atttempted to reproduce the style, but not until the end of the 5th century did their products find much of a place even in their local markets.

1. **Early Classical Attic Red Figure:** *c.* 480–*c.* 450 B.C.

   Background: Shiny black.
   Colour of Designs: Orange-red.
   Decoration: Decoration tended to divide into four schools:
   a. Imitators of the grandeur of free painting.
   b. Classicists, who adapted new types and groupings.
   c. Miniaturists.
   d. Mannerists, who continued to use or reinterpret Archaic forms.
   Generally decoration lacked spontaneity and tended to be studied, and drawing was emphasized to the point where the pot became less important than the painting on it. Artistic quality declined but drawing became more accomplished–especially the drawing of the human figure and folds of drapery, the latter being shown more sketchily with less emphasis on formal folds.
   Repertory of Designs: Primarily human figures, now regularly with the profile eye. Three-quarter faces and shading appeared. Ornaments included lotus and palmette (often large and elaborate, and sometimes straggly).
   Painters and Potters: The Pan Painter, the Pistoxenos Painter, the Achilles Painter, the Penthesileia Painter, the Sotades Painter and the Niobid Painter.
   Shapes of Pots: Tended to become slimmer–and the transition from one part to another less sharply defined. Shapes included the neck amphora, pelike, stamnos, hydria, column-krater, bell-krater, calyx-krater, volute-krater, oinochoi, stemless cup, skyphos, lekythos, squat lekythos, and alabastron.
   Clay: Fine orange-red.

2. **Classical Attic Red Figure:** *c.* 450–*c.* 425 B.C.

   Background: Shiny black.
   Colour of Designs: Red-orange.

Decoration: Decoration was based on the portrayal of effortless human dignity in quiet standing or sitting poses; even scenes of battles or of satyrs were toned down. Perspective was only used for tables and chairs. The general effect is not of painted pottery, but of pottery with painting on it. Most effort was devoted to a central scene on the front, the back having two or three stock figures. The relief line became rare; dilute lines and shading were used more.
Repertory of Designs: Similar to Early Classical Red Figure.
Painters and Potters: The Achilles Painter, Polygnotos, and the Eretria Painter.
Clay: Fine, red-orange.

3. Late Classical Attic Red Figure: *c.* 425–*c.* 400 B.C.

Background: Shiny black.
Colour of Designs: Red-orange with white, gold.
Decoration: Figures tended to leave the plane of the pot in perspective depth or emerge from the field. More attention was given to rounded forms and subtle curves of contour. The emphatic relief line and sharp outline were abandoned. Poses tended to be theatrical and expressions vapidly intense.
Repertory of Designs: Limited.
Painters and Potters: The Dinos Painter, the Meidias Painter.
Shapes of Pots: Tended to be more swelling with emphasis on moulding of foot and lip. Shapes included the pelike, bell-krater, calyx-krater, oinochoe, stemmed cup, squat and tall lekythoi, loutrophoros and lekanis.

4. Fourth Century Attic Red Figure: *c.* 400–323 B.C.

Background: Shiny black.
Colour of Designs: Red-orange, yellow-brown, white, yellow.
Decoration: Decoration became a minor art. Drapery was shaded and later human figures were also shaded. Full profile figures became rare. Scenes became crowded. Perspective was attempted by placing figures in tiers. Gradually work became more clumsy. Backs of pots almost always had a pair or trio of cloaked youths very poorly done.
Repertory of Designs: Similar to early periods with more use of hooks, stars, stripes and little animals on drapery, as well as use of garlands of leaves and berries. Dionysus and Aphrodite were the favourite figures along with Amazons, Arimaspians and griffins.
Painters and Potters: The Talos Painter and the Jena Painter.
Shapes of Pots: Tended to become more and more elongated. The

favourite shape was the pelike, followed by the bell-krater, calyx-krater, hydria and skyphos.

Clay: Fine, red-orange.

5. Classical Corinthian Red Figure: *c.* 400–*c.* 323 B.C.

Corinthian potters imitated the Attic Red Figure pottery. Their imitations may be distinguished primarily by the *clay*, which is yellowish. The *better quality* has an *orange slip*, sometimes with a red wash on reserved areas; the relief line was used freely. The *poorer quality* had a *red wash*, but no slip.

6. Classical Boeotian Red Figure: *c.* 460–*c.* 350 B.C.

Boeotian imitations of Attic Red Figure pottery were poor. Depiction of human anatomy was flat and drapery poorly drawn. The clay was paler than Attic and the paint less even.

7. Classical Etruscan Red Figure: *c.* 400–323 B.C.

Etruscan imitations of Attic Red Figure pottery are distinguished by a paler clay, which fired to a light brown. Painting was often by the application of colour *over* the black (instead of the outlining and reserving of the figure in red against a black background). Details were normally incised.

Later the true reserving Red Figure technique was used, but the relief line was seldom employed.

Still later, flowers began to appear in perspective, scenes were taken from the Etruscan tradition rather than the Greek, so that hideous and grotesque demons were common. Other decoration included bands of full tongues (each in a rounded compartment), trefoil leaves, palmettes with leaves only remaining a fringe, and frames of spiral hooks. Output was small and little was exported.

8. Classical South Italian Red Figure: *c.* 450–*c.* 323 B.C.

South Italian imitators of Attic Red Figure were numerous:

a. *Owl-Pillar Group* (*c.* 450 B.C.): apparently made in Campania, probably by immigrants from Athens; a clumsy, ill-proportioned style.

b. *Campanian and Sicilian* (*c.* 375–*c.* 300 B.C.): various styles developed in Campania and Sicily; generally they tended to become ornate and gaudy, using many colours. Yellow and white were used heavily on figures and floral ornament. The style of drawing was stiff and straight. Ornaments included rows of spiral hooks and dot rosettes. The clay was often light brown with or without a reddish coating. The paint tended to blister.

c. *Lucanian or Group A* (*c.* 450–*c.* 300 B.C.): apparently made west of Tarentum, was monotonous, stiff and angular, though often amusing in its conscious or unconscious parody of Attic painting. The stock formula was a three-figure group (women being pursued or satyrs with maenads) on the front and two or three draped youths on the back. Characteristic designs included a doubled dark stripe down women's skirts, palmettes with serrated edges, Z-patterns and thick rays.

d. *Apulian or Group B* (*c.* 430–*c.* 290 B.C.): apparently made at Tarentum. This pottery quickly became grandiose. Though individual figures were well drawn in statuesque poses, the total composition was clumsy. Scenes were usually mythological, featuring Dionysiac rites, women, and Eros; and often tragic, with funeral scenes being common. Both fronts and backs of pots showed scenes. Scenes were in two or three levels. Vacant spaces were filled by sashes, rosettes, flowers (crisp, metallic and in three-quarters view), meanders (modelled by shading) and palmettes. White, yellow and purple paint were used broadly over the dark paint.

e. *Paestan* (*c.* 370–323 B.C.): made at Paestum. The bell-krater was the favourite shape, straight-sided with a square picture framed at the sides by a reserved line, or the typical Paestan volute and palmettes. Typical themes were Dionysiac or dramatic scenes from plays and mythology on the front, and a pair of cloaked youths on the back. Drapery was often decorated with a row of squares or dots along the edge. Though white and yellow were used, the style was not ornate.

General: The technique of South Italian Red Figure was often equal to Attic technique. Composition was usually poorer. The clay varied; sometimes it resembled Attic, but was duller or paler; at other times it was yellowish, resembling Corinthian, or chocolate. A reddish wash was common. The paint was often muddy or greenish with a harsh metallic sheen (unlike the glassy transparency of the Attic sheen); it tended to flake or blister.

Classical Designs

SOUTH ITALIAN RED FIGURE STYLES: 450–323 B.C.

A. LUCANIAN STYLES

Fig. A-12
c. 340 B.C.

Fig. A-13
c. 340 B.C.

B. APULIAN STYLES

Fig. A-14
c. 330 B.C.

(*after Fig. 52 in
A. Furtwängler and
K. Reichhold's*
Griechische
Vasenmalerei *II*)

Classical Designs (*contd.*)

SOUTH ITALIAN RED FIGURE STYLES: 450–323 B.C. (*contd.*)

C. PAESTAN STYLES

Fig. A-15
Late 4th century B.C.

(*based on an illustration from R. M. Cook's* Greek Painted Pottery, *Methuen, and reproduced with their kind permission*)

VIII Hellenistic Pottery (*c.* 350–146 B.C.)

1. **West Slope Ware:** *c.* 323–146 B.C. (East of the Adriatic)

Background: Dark, irregular, dull, muddy and streaky.
Colour of Designs: White, yellow and gold.
Decoration: Painting in colour was done on top of the dark background paint. Decoration was limited to the upper part of pots. Style was rough and coarse.
Repertory of Designs: Human figures were rare. Designs included: ivy, hanging buds, laurel, vines, necklaces with pendants, rows of spiral hooks, chequers (plain or coloured), boxed and cross-hatched rectangles, rosettes and rough stars.
Shapes of Pots: Solid, clumsy, and ill-proportioned: squat neck amphorae with twisted handles, kantharoi, saucers, plates, bowls, cups, kraters, oinochoai; plastic ornaments were common on handles with ribs and moulding on bodies.
Clay: Varied, but less fine than Red Figure clay.

2. **Gnathian:** *c.* 350–250 B.C. (Italy)

Background: Dark.
Colour of Designs: White, yellow and purple.
Decoration: Decoration was deliberately pretty and made too much use of filler ornaments.
Repertory of Designs: Wreaths, scrolls of ivy and vine, bands of laurel, necklaces, ribbons, female heads, full figures of women and Eros, actors' masks, musical instruments and birds.
Shapes of Pots: Elegant, including the krater, pelike, oinochoe, skyphos, kantharos, squat lekythos, bottle, bowl and cup; ribbing was common.
Clay: Varied widely.

3. **Lagynos Group:** *c.* 150 B.C. (East of the Adriatic)

Background: Light; hard white slip.
Colour of Designs: Black, brown, yellowish-brown with some sheen.
Decoration: Decoration was normally simple and restricted to the shoulder. Style was hasty, but good.
Repertory of Designs: Ivy, laurel, festoons, wreaths, musical instruments, and dolphins–occasionally words.
Shapes of Pots: The lagynos (a squat angular high-necked pitcher)

was characteristic; a few pyxides were also produced. Walls of pots were often very thin.

Clay: Moderately fine and micaceous, varied from light brown to reddish.

4. **Hadra Ware:** *c.* 260–*c.* 210 B.C. (Alexandria)

Background: Yellowish slip or chalky white coat.

Colour of Designs: Dark paint, brown to black, was used on the *yellowish slip*. Polychrome painting was used on the *chalky white coat*, including: reds, blues, yellows and greens in tempera (i.e. not fast colours).

Decoration: The *yellow slip type* had a major field of decoration on the top of the belly, and two minor fields of decoration on the neck and shoulder (the lower belly was reserved and the foot was dark). Figures were in silhouette and rarely outlined; incision was common; white was used for ornaments. Painting was sober and neat.

The *chalky white coat type* usually was decorated with festoons across the neck or belly. Painting was crude.

Repertory of Designs: Yellow slip type: laurel and ivy wreaths, volutes, scrolls, wilting palmettes, garlands, dolphins, long-necked birds, rosettes, panels with cross-hatching or opposed triangles. Figures of confronting animals or monsters and hunting scenes sometimes appeared.

Chalky white coat type: thick festoons, insignia of sex (arms for men, toilet articles for women).

Shapes of Pots: Hydria only, though shapes varied. The chalky white coat polychrome type was used in funerals as container for ashes.

Clay: Light brown to reddish.

5. **Canosa Ware:** Late 4th to 3rd centuries B.C. (Canosa in Northern Apulia, Italy)

Background: White slip.

Colour of Designs: Yellow, pink, red and blue.

Decoration: The white slip and the colours of the decoration were put on the pots after firing. Scenes depicted human and animal figures drawn in outline on dark paint–and often filled with a yellowish wash. Inner detail was indicated by a few dark lines or touches of colour. The white background was usually painted over in pink or blue. The style was flat.

Repertory of Designs: Human and animal figures (winged or wing-less horses) with floral patterns subordinated. Rosettes were used as filling ornaments.

10

Shapes of Pots: Askos crowded with plastic forms, oinochoe with long slender neck, kantharos.
Clay: Fairly fine, light brown.

6. **Centuripae Ware:** Early Hellenistic (interior of Sicily)

Background: Chalky white undercoat often covered with pink or (on early pieces) black.
Colour of Designs: Polychrome-black, browns, yellows, reds, blues, all very friable.
Decoration: Figures were painted, after firing of the pot, in black outline over the chalky white undercoat, and then filled in with a choice of colours. Figures, usually women, were spaced in studied poses that were usually neither fully frontal nor fully profile, and were modelled by shading and highlights and coloured to simulate nature.
Repertory of Designs: Figures of women. Plastic ornament left little space for other decoration.
Shapes of Pots: Bell-kraters with high lids and pedestals but no handles, lowish bowls with tall conical lids, and skyphoi. All were large.
Clay: Coarse, red to brown.

Appendix 2

SHAPES AND USES OF GREEK POTTERY
(DETAILED ACCOUNT)

Shapes and Uses of Greek Pottery
(Detailed Account)

The present appendix is designed to provide an expansion of the simplified data presented in Part 4.

For the amateur, shapes can have a special fascination, even when all he has in hand is a relatively small potsherd. By its contour, thickness and the slight ridges of the potter's wheel, he often can come to a conclusion as to the shape of the whole pot. The extremely thin-walled fragments of a Corinthian skyphos, for example, can be identified readily. The base and a portion of a stem are sufficient to establish that the whole was kylix. A neck may be enough to prove that it once belonged to an aryballos. Another fragment may be quickly recognized as part of a lamp.

It may be worth remarking that, in contrast to the pottery of other countries which is usually formed in continuous curves, Greek pottery often was strongly articulated. Mouth, neck, body and foot usually were set off from one another. The result, however, was completely harmonious.

Each piece was an individual creation, there being no mass-production of identical items. On the other hand, the number of forms was limited. Variations occurred, of course; some were relatively major ones in terms of size and contour, others were subtle. In general, sturdy shapes tended to become more refined, more elongated and more graceful; they also became ever more adapted to their particular use.

As certain descriptive terms are used in this appendix, the following pages provide a key for quick reference.

Key to Terms Used in Describing Shapes

TYPES OF MOUTH OR LIP

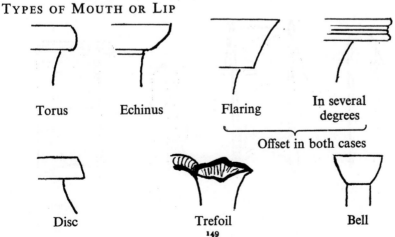

Torus   Echinus   Flaring   In several degrees

Offset in both cases

Disc   Trefoil   Bell

TYPES OF FOOT

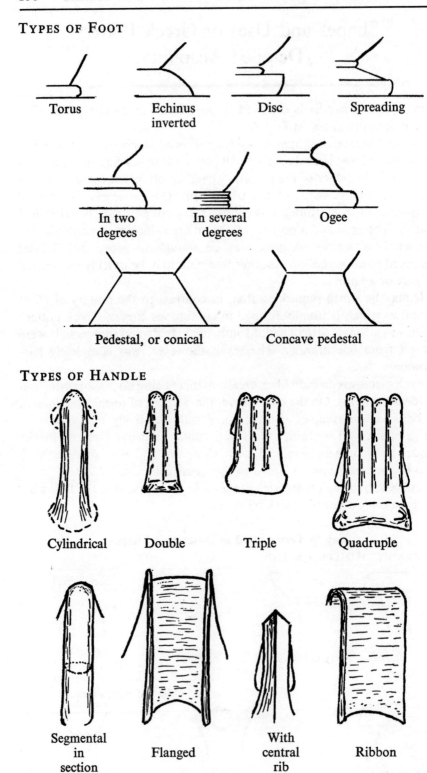

Torus   Echinus inverted   Disc   Spreading

In two degrees   In several degrees   Ogee

Pedestal, or conical   Concave pedestal

TYPES OF HANDLE

Cylindrical   Double   Triple   Quadruple

Segmental in section   Flanged   With central rib   Ribbon

TYPES OF HANDLE (*contd.*)

Volute   Twisted

1 Amphorae

Definition: Amphora: a tall, two-handled pot with a neck considerably narrower than the body.

Uses: A. Coarse, narrow-mouthed, plugged amphorae were used for storage and transport of provisions–oil, wine, olives, etc.

B. Very large, outsize amphorae were used for funerals and as grave-markers.

C. Fine, painted, wide-mouthed amphorae were used as decanters.

D. Other finely painted amphorae were used for special purposes such as prizes at festivals, grave offerings, etc.

Height: Varied considerably:

Large Geometric amphorae:	about 155 cm. or	5 ft.
Normal amphorae:	about 45 cm. or	18 in.
Small amphorae:	about 30 cm. or	12 in.

Types:

A. Neck Amphorae		**B. One-piece Amphorae**	
1. Geometric	900–700 B.C.	1. Attic 7th century–323 B.C.	
2. Proto-Attic	710–610 B.C.	a. 'Type Ia'	610–425 B.C.
3. Attic	600–323 B.C.	b. 'Type Ib'	550–450 B.C.
a. 'Type IIa'	530–450 B.C.	c. 'Type Ic'	575–550 and
a. (1) Nolan	Mid 5th century B.C.		520–470 B.C.
b. 'Type IIb'	500 to mid 4th century B.C.	d. Pelike	520 to 4th century B.C.
c. 'Type IIc' Panathenaic	560 into 3rd century B.C.		
d. 'Type IId' Pointed	5th century B.C.		
e. Stamnos	525–323 B.C.		
f. Loutrophoros	525–323 B.C.		
g. Nikosthenic & Villanovan	7th–6th centuries B.C.		
h. Volute			

SILHOUETTES OF MAIN TYPES

Scale: 1 cm. = 10 cm.

A. Neck Amphorae

The neck meets the body on this type at a sharp angle. The form was common from the Geometric period up to the period of decline of Greek pottery.

1. *Geometric Neck Amphora:* characteristic form 900–700 B.C.

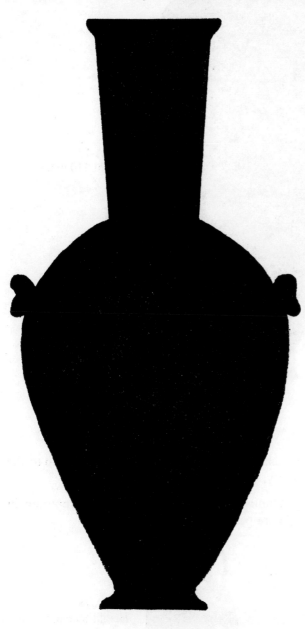

Fig. A-16
Height 155 cm.

2. *Proto-Attic Neck Amphora:* characteristic form 710–610 B.C.

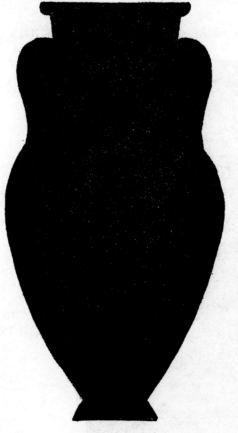

Fig. A-17
Height 110 cm.

3. *Attic Neck Amphora:* characteristic form from 6th century up to the decline of Greek pottery.

    a. 'Type IIa': *Lip* echinus-shaped, *foot* torus-shaped, common in the Late Black Figure period, 530–450 B.C.

Fig. A-18
Height 39 cm.

a. (1) Nolan Type: So-called from Nola in South Italy where many fine examples have been found. Earlier examples have triple handles, and later examples usually have a central ridge running up the handle. Popular in Red Figure pottery from the first half of the 5th century into the second half of the 5th century B.C.

Fig. A-19
Height 33 cm.

b. 'Type IIb': *Body* elongated, *handles* twisted, *mouth* in two degrees, the lower echinus-shaped, *foot* in two degrees, the lower convex, *ridge* at base of body. Common from about 500 to the 4th century B.C.

Fig. A-20
Height 35 cm.

c. 'Type IIc' or Panathenaic Amphora: Finely painted in the Black Figure Style, these amphorae were filled with oil and presented to winners at the Panathenaic Festivals. Though the shape was not confined to prize vessels, only these bore the inscription 'from the games at Athens'. *Body* broad and tapering sharply downward, *handles* cylindrical. Given out from 560 well into the 3rd century B.C.

Fig. A-21
Height 70 cm.

d. 'Type IId' or Pointed Amphora: *Body* pointed so that it could be set in a stand, *handles* cylindrical, ridge at base of neck. Popular in 5th century B.C.

Fig. A-22
Height 56 cm.

e. Stamnos: Evidence for use of the name stamnos is insufficient, but it has been retained for convenience in identifying this particular shape. *Neck* reduced to a mere collar, *shoulders* high, *handles* set horizontally. Common from the last quarter of the 6th century up to the decline of Greek pottery.

Fig. A-23
Height 33 cm.

f. Loutrophoros: A special type of amphora used at weddings and funerals of unmarried persons. *Neck* very tall and funnel-shaped, *body* slender, *mouth* flaring. Common from the late 6th century up to the decline of Greek pottery.

Note: The loutrophoros usually was an amphora, but sometimes the form appears as a hydria with three handles.

Fig. A-24
Height 84 cm.

Fig. A-25
Height 75 cm.

g. Nikosthenic and Villanovan Amphorae: Nikosthenic pottery (named after the potter) was produced in Athens, primarily for the Etruscan market in the late 6th century B.C.

Villanovan pottery of similar shape was produced in Italy during the Early Archaic period.

Both had a conical neck which at its base was nearly as wide as the body. Vertical broad ribbon-handles joined on to the lip.

Fig. A-26
Nikosthenic amphora
c. 520–515 B.C.
Height 38·5 cm.

h. Volute Amphora.

Fig. A-27
Height including
handles
28·5 cm.

B. One-piece Amphorae

The neck and body merge in an unbroken curve. This type first appeared in the 7th century B.C. and lasted until the decline of Greek pottery.

1. *Attic One-piece Amphora*

a. 'Type Ia': *Lip* flaring and straight or slightly curved, *foot* inverted echinus shape, *handles* cylindrical. This type was common from the late 7th century until the third quarter of the 5th century B.C.

Fig. A-28
Height 55 cm.

b. 'Type Ib': *Lip* flaring and slightly concave, *foot* in two parts with the lower part convex. This type was common from the mid 6th century to about 450 B.C.

Fig. A-29
Height 51 cm.

c. 'Type Ic': *Mouth* convex and spreading, *foot* either torus or echinus-shaped. This type was popular in Black Figure pottery in the second quarter of the 6th century and in Red Figure pottery from about 520 to 470 B.C.

Fig. A-30
Height 40 cm.

d. Pelike: The name pelike was applied by early archaeologists to the one-piece amphora with a sagging belly and broad neck. In fact, the name appears to have no justification, but is retained for convenience. The form first appeared about 520 B.C. and lasted until the 4th century B.C.

Fig. A-31
Height 41 cm.

2 Hydriai

Definition: Hydria: a pot with a vertical handle at the back and two horizontal handles at the sides.
Use: For fetching water.
Height: 30–45 cm. or 12–18 in. was normal, but some are larger and some smaller.
Types: A. Neck Hydria   7th to 6th century B.C.
        B. One-piece Hydria   End of 6th century to 4th century B.C.

SILHOUETTES OF MAIN TYPES
Scale: 1 cm. = 10 cm.

A. Neck Hydriai
The neck meets the body at a sharp angle. The form was in common use from the 7th century to the 6th century B.C.

1. *Early Hydria: Belly* wide, *shoulder* broadly rounded, *side handles* set horizontally, but pointing upward, *vertical handle* attached to rim of mouth, *neck* off-set, *foot* torus-shaped with pedestal. Found in Attic, Cycladic and Corinthian pottery.

Fig. A-32
Height 52 cm.

2. *Sixth Century Hydria*

Fig. A-33
Similar to early type except *side handles* set lower and pointing outward, *foot* echinus-shaped
Second quarter of 6th century B.C.
Height 34 cm.

Fig. A-34
Shoulder flatter joining belly
in a sharp curve or even an
angle, *foot* echinus-shaped
Found in Attic, Corinthian,
Laconian, Chalcidian and
Caeretan pottery
Mid 6th century B.C.
Height 55 cm.

Fig. A-35
Shoulder even flatter, joining
belly at an angle, *body* more
elongated, *foot* disc or torus-
shaped, *vertical handle*
attachments imitate metal
technique
Attic type
Last quarter of
6th century B.C.
Height 46 cm.

B. One-piece Hydriai

This type of hydria is often called a *kalpis* by archaeologists, but there
appears to be no justification for this from ancient literature where the
two terms hydria and kalpis were used interchangeably. It appears that
the word kalpis was poetic and possibly Aeolian in origin. The one-piece
hydria appeared at about the end of the 6th century and lasted until the
4th century B.C.

Fig. A-36
Body wider than high,
mouth convex, *foot* disc-
shaped, *handle* joins neck
below the mouth
c. 500 B.C.
Height 36 cm.

Fig. A-37
Body similarly wide,
shoulder more angular,
lip concave,
foot echinus-shaped
c. 470 B.C.
Height 40 cm.

Fig. A-38
Body narrower, *foot* less
wide and higher and in
several degrees
c. 430 B.C.
Height 42 cm.

Fig. A-39
Neck higher, *body* more
elongated, *side handles* have
accentuated curves,
mouth more flaring
c. 350 B.C.
Height 29 cm.

3 Oinochoai

Definition: Oinochoe: a jug or pitcher with one vertical handle at the back. It is one of the commonest and most varied forms of Greek pottery.

Mouth may be trefoil, round or beaked.
Neck may be straight or curved, narrow or broad.
Body may be slim, squat, truncated or angular.

Use: For pouring wine.

Height: The early oinochoai compared in size to the amphorae. After the early 6th century, they were usually about 30 cm. or 12 inches or so high; some were smaller throughout.

Types:

A.	'Standard' Oinochoai	8th and 7th centuries B.C.
B.	Attic Oinochoai	6th century B.C. to decline of Greek pottery.
C.	Bell-mouthed Oinochoai	Late Geometric into 7th century B.C.
D.	Broad-bottomed Oinochoai	7th century into Hellenistic period.
E.	Others	

SILHOUETTES OF MAIN TYPES

Scale: 1 cm. = 10 cm.

A. 'Standard' Oinochoai

More or less ovoid body, wide neck and trefoil mouth.

Fig. A-40
'Standard' oinochoe
8th century
Height 33·4 cm.

Fig. A-41
'Standard' oinochoe
7th century
Height 40 cm.

B. Attic Oinochoai

1. *Proto-Attic Oinochoai*

Fig. A-42
775–750 B.C.
Height 20 cm.

2. *Attic Black Figure and Red Figure Oinochoai*

a. 'Type I': *Body* slender, one-piece, *mouth* trefoil or round, *handle* high or level with mouth. This type of slender oinochoe with a sagging belly has sometimes been called an *olpe* by archaeologists, but the distinction is not borne out in the ancient writings. Common in Black Figure pottery, but rare in Red Figure Style.

Fig. A-43
Height 32 cm.

Fig. A-44
Height 26 cm.

b. 'Type II': *Body* slender, *shoulder* set off slightly from body. Common in both Black Figure and Red Figure Styles.

Fig. A-45
Height 23 cm.

c. 'Type III': *Body* bulbous, one-piece, often small, *mouth* trefoil, *foot* low and curved or echinus-shaped, *handles* low and cylindrical or flat or with a central rib. This type often is very small. Popular in the late 5th and 4th centuries B.C.

Fig. A-46
Height 24 cm.

d. 'Type IV': *Body* bulbous, *neck* off-set, *mouth* round.

Fig. A-47
Height 19 cm.

e. 'Type V': *Body* bulbous, *neck* off-set, *mouth* trefoil.

Fig. A-48
Height 42 cm.

f. Other Attic types:

Fig. A-49
Note beaked spout with disc
at each side. *Neck* off-set,
handle flanged,
foot echinus-shaped
End of 6th century B.C.
Height 25·5 cm.

Fig. A-50
Spout also beaked,
handle high with disc at base
of handle and spout,
foot ogee
Second half of 5th century B.C.
Height 20·5 cm.

Fig. A-51
Spout beaked, *handle* lower,
shoulder sharply set off from
body, *foot* none
Late 5th or
early 4th century B.C.
Height 13 cm.

C. Bell-mouthed Oinochoai

Fig. A-52
Late Attic Geometric,
8th century B.C.
Often these oinochoai were
very large and peculiar
in shape
Height 80 cm.

Fig. A-53
Sub-Geometric East Greek
'Wild Goat' Style,
7th century B.C.
Height 30 cm.

Fig. A-54
Proto-Corinthian,
650–625 B.C.
Height 20·5 cm.

D. Broad-bottomed Oinochoai

Fig. A-55
Conical oinochoe: *Mouth*
trefoil, *neck* narrow,
body consists of little more
than a broad conical shoulder
Proto-Corinthian, 700–600 B.C.
Height 23 cm.

Fig. A-56
Typical broad-bottomed
oinochoe: Low, *body* broad,
sides nearly vertical,
neck relatively narrow,
mouth trefoil
Proto-Corinthian, 675–650 B.C.
Height 11 cm.

Fig. A-57
'Lagynos': A Hellenistic form
of broad-bottomed oinochoe,
shoulder sharp and curving,
mouth round
Late 3rd or 2nd century B.C.
Height 20 cm.

E. Other Oinochoai

Fig. A-58
Cycladic oinochoe
700–650 B.C.
Height 40 cm.

Fig. A-59
Rhodian oinochoe
675–650 B.C.
Height 16 cm.

4 Kraters

Definition: Krater: a deep bowl with a wide mouth.
Use: For mixing wine with water.
Height: Usually 30–45 cm. or 12–18 inches.
Types: A. Simple Kraters   Proto-Geometric to Geometric periods.

B. Kotyle Kraters   Early Attic 650–600 B.C. and East Greek 'Wild Goat' 650–500 B.C.

C. Column Kraters   625–425 B.C.

D. Volute Kraters   600–323 B.C.

E. Calyx Kraters   550 B.C. to decline of Greek painted pottery.

F. Bell Kraters   Early 5th century to decline of Greek painted pottery.

G. Kalathos

SILHOUETTES OF MAIN TYPES

Scale: 1 cm. = 10 cm.

A. Simple Krater

Fig. A-60
Attic Geometric krater
with lid
Late 9th century B.C.
Height 57 cm.

Fig. A-61
Simple Proto-Attic krater
c. 700–675 B.C.
Height 27 cm.

1. In the Proto-Geometric period, the krater was sturdy and wide with a low belly and modest foot (which later became conical). Handles were horizontal and often doubled.
2. In the Geometric period, the shape became tenser and the body curved strongly to the simple lip. The foot was low or stemmed to a flaring pedestal. Handles often were joined to the lip by a sort of strap.
3. Very large Late Geometric funerary kraters had a short vertical neck and the handles did not reach the lip.

B. Kotyle Krater

1. A giant kotyle krater, usually attached to a high flaring pedestal and covered with a lid, was popular in Attic pottery from about 750–700 B.C.

Fig. A-62
Attic giant kotyle krater
c. 750–700 B.C.
Height 100 cm.

2. The kotyle type krater, with or without the pedestal, was popular in Attic pottery and in the East Greek 'Wild Goat' Style of pottery 650–500 B.C., as well as in other styles.

Fig. A-63
'Wild Goat' kotyle krater
c. 675–650 B.C.
Height 17 cm.

Fig. A-64
Proto-Corinthian kotyle krater
c. 800–750 B.C.
Height 26 cm.

Fig. A-65
Etruscan krater
c. 650 B.C.
Height 36 cm.

C. Column Krater

The column krater is so-called from the columnar shape of the handles. Each handle consists of a pair of cylindrical stems terminating in a horizontal rectangular plate joined to the rim of the mouth. The broad lip is concave in outline and hangs over the neck. This type was popular in Corinth from the last quarter of the 7th century onwards. In Attica, its popularity began only in the first half of the 6th century. The form lost popularity in the third quarter of the 5th century B.C.

Fig. A-66
Chalcidian column krater
c. 550–530 B.C.
Height 45·7 cm.

D. Volute Krater

The volute krater gets its name from the shape of its handles, each of which is in the form of a spiral with flanged sides. Generally the shape is common from about 600 B.C., but it did not become popular in Attic pottery until the first half of the 6th century; it lasted until the decline of Greek painted pottery.

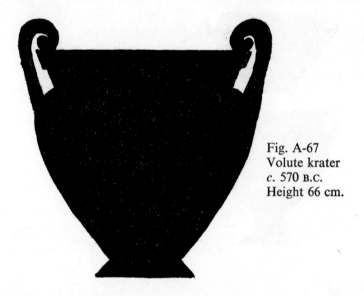

Fig. A-67
Volute krater
c. 570 B.C.
Height 66 cm.

E. Calyx Krater

The calyx krater's name is based also on its shape: it resembles the calyx of a flower. The body is in two parts, the lower convex and the upper concave. Handles are set at the top of the lower part. In Attic pottery the handles curve upward. There is no neck. The foot in Attic pottery is in two degrees with a ridge at the base of the body. Other types sometimes have straight horizontal handles and a conical foot. (Note: in profile this type of calyx krater resembles the Chiot chalice, a cup–see Fig. A-111. The krater, however, is much larger and was used for mixing wine and water, while the chalice was for drinking.) The calyx krater appeared in about the middle of the 6th century–in Attica, not until the end of the 6th century where it was very popular in the Red Figure Style–and lasted until the decline of Greek painted pottery.

Fig. A-68
Attic calyx krater
c. 500 B.C.
Height 34 cm.

Fig. A-69
Attic calyx krater
460–450 B.C.
Height 54 cm.

F. Bell Krater

In the form of an inverted bell, this type of krater has loop handles which curve upward placed high on the body; later downcurving lugs replaced the loop handles. The form appeared in the early 5th century and continued in use until the decline of Greek painted pottery.

Fig. A-70
Bell krater with upcurving handles
c. 450 B.C.
Height 38 cm.

Fig. A-71
Bell krater with downcurving lugs in place of handles
c. 470 B.C.
Height 37 cm.

G. Kalathos

The kalathos is a type of krater with slightly flaring sides and with a spout on one side near the base. The name is derived from its shape, which is similar to the ancient Greek wool basket. The shape is rare.

Fig. A-72
c. 480–470 B.C.
Height 52 cm.

5 Lekythoi*

Definition: Lekythos: a one-handled jug with a narrow neck and deep mouth.

Use: For oil, unguents and as offering for the dead.

Height: 7–35 cm. or 3–14 inches.

Types:
A. Early Lekythoi — Proto-Geometric to Archaic periods.
B. One-piece Lekythoi — First half of 6th century B.C.
C. Neck Lekythoi — Mid 6th century to 5th century B.C.
D. Squat Lekythoi — Mid 5th century to decline of Greek pottery.

SILHOUETTES OF MAIN TYPES†

Scales: 1 cm. = 5 cm. and 1 cm. = 10 cm

A. Early Lekythoi

Scales: 1 cm. = 5 cm.   1 cm. = 10 cm.

Fig. A-73
Proto-Geometric lekythos
Height 15 cm.

B. One-piece Lekythoi

The one-piece lekythoi had a continuous curve from neck to base. This was the characteristic form of lekythos in Attic and Corinthian pottery during the first half of the 6th century B.C.

Scales: 1 cm. = 5 cm.   1 cm. = 10 cm.

---

* The word lekythos had a wide meaning in ancient Greece, probably generally meaning all oil jugs, including the athletes' oil bottle (now called aryballos) as well as the types now given this name by archaeologists (listed in this section).

† Certain lekythoi resemble certain oinochoai superficially, at a first glance. Oinochoai, however, were wine-pitchers and were in most cases larger than the lekythoi, which were small jugs for oil, perfumes, etc.

Fig. A-74
One-piece Attic lekythos.
Egg-shaped body, concave
mouth, plastic ring at base
of neck
Second quarter of
6th century B.C.
Height 17 cm.

C. Neck Lekythoi

In this type the shoulder was set off from the body and the neck was set off from the shoulder. The form appeared in Attic pottery in about the middle of the 6th century and was common throughout the 5th century B.C.

Scales: 1 cm. = 5 cm.   1 cm. = 10 cm.

Fig. A-75
Neck lekythos. Slim body,
angular shoulder, no ring
at neck
c. 440 B.C.
Height 30 cm.

D. Squat Lekythoi

The squat lekythoi are broad at the base and have no distinct shoulder. The form was popular in Attic pottery during the second half of the 5th century and up to the decline of Greek pottery.

Scales: 1 cm. = 5 cm.   1 cm. = 10 cm.

Fig.-76
Squat lekythos
410–400 B.C.
Height 20 cm.

6 Aryballoi

Definition: Aryballos: oil bottle with a narrow neck.
Use: Commonly used by athletes at the baths.
Height: 5–13 cm. or 2–5 inches.
Types: A. 'Corinthian'   725–323 B.C.
   B. 'Attic'   700–323 B.C.

SILHOUETTES OF MAIN TYPES

Scales: 1 cm. = 5 cm. and 1 cm. = 10 cm.

A. 'Corinthian' Aryballoi

The 'Corinthian' aryballos had a round body, a broad disc-shaped mouth and, generally, one handle. This shape was common in Corinthian pottery from the beginning of the Archaic period to the decline of Greek pottery (725–323 B.C.). In Attica it enjoyed a brief vogue, 550–520 B.C.

Scales: 1 cm. = 5 cm.   1 cm. = 10 cm.

Fig. A-77
Early 'Corinthian' aryballos
725–700 B.C.
Height 7·5 cm.

Fig. A-78
'Corinthian' aryballos
c. 550 B.C.
Height 8 cm.

B. 'Attic' Aryballoi

The 'Attic' type of aryballos had a hemispherical or bell-shaped mouth and two handles with projections (some of the later versions had no handles). It was common from 700 to 323 B.C.

Scales: 1 cm. = 5 cm.   1 cm. = 10 cm.

Fig. A-79
'Attic' aryballos
Early 5th century B.C.
Height 9 cm.

7 Alabastra

Definition: Alabastron: an elongated narrow-necked small vase with no handles, but sometimes with string holes or lugs.
Use: Used as a perfume container.
Height: 7–20 cm. or 3–8 inches.

SILHOUETTES OF MAIN TYPES

Scales: 1 cm. = 5 cm. and 1 cm. = 10 cm.

The alabastron was a typical Corinthian shape, but was also produced in Attica (sometimes with two small ears or lugs) and in a long pointed version in East Greek, Etruscan and Italo-Corinthian pottery. The shape was common from 700 to 323 B.C.

Scales: 1 cm. = 5 cm.   1 cm. = 10 cm.

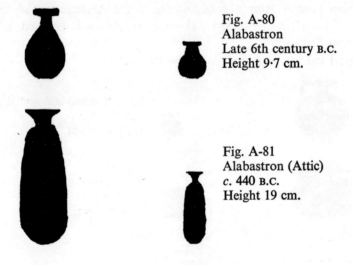

Fig. A-80
Alabastron
Late 6th century B.C.
Height 9·7 cm.

Fig. A-81
Alabastron (Attic)
c. 440 B.C.
Height 19 cm.

8 Askoi

Definition: Askos: a small flask with a circular body, wider than it was high, with a convex top and arched handle reaching from one side across the top to a spout on the other side.

Use: Used for containing oil.

Diameter: 5–15 cm. or 2–6 inches.

SILHOUETTES OF MAIN TYPES

Askoi varied in shape. Thus East Greek askoi tended to be lumpy, flat-bottomed and large (*c.* 15 cm. in diameter). Apulian and other Italian askoi were deep and bulky, with a body like a brooding hen. Large, round-bottomed askoi are found in Apulian and Canosan pottery. Attic and Corinthian askoi were very low, neat, flat-bottomed and small (*c.* 10 cm. in diameter). The form was common from 700 to 323 B.C.

Scales: 1 cm. = 5 cm.   1 cm. = 10 cm.

Fig. A-82
Attic askos
c. 430 B.C.
Diameter 8 cm.

9 Pyxides

Definition: Pyxis: a round box, usually without handles.
    Use: To hold cosmetics or trinkets.
   Size: Most common about 10 cm. or 4 inches across.
 Types: A. Globular Pyxis   Proto-Geometric.
        B. Pointed Pyxis   Early Geometric.
        C. Flat Pyxis   Late Geometric.
        D. Tall Convex Pyxis Proto-Corinthian.
        E. Straight-sided Pyxis 8th century Corinthian.
        F. 'Type I': Tripod Pyxis
                      6th century Attic.
        G. 'Type II': Low Concave-sided Pyxis
                      Late 5th and 4th century Attic.
        H. 'Type III': High Concave-sided Pyxis
                      7th century Attic and Corinthian.
        I. 'Type IV': Normal or Cylindrical Pyxis
                      4th century Attic and Corinthian.

SILHOUETTES OF MAIN TYPES

Scale: 1 cm. = 10 cm.

A. Globular Pyxis

The Globular pyxis had a globular body with an out-turned lip and low foot. It was a Proto-Geometric form.

Fig. A-83
Height 25 cm.

B. Pointed Pyxis

The pointed pyxis ended below in a point. It dates from the Early Geometric period.

Fig. A-84
Height 16 cm.

C. Flat Pyxis

The Late Geometric pyxis was flat in shape with a cover.

Fig. A-85
8th century B.C.
Diameter 20 cm.

D. Tall Convex Pyxis

Proto-Corinthian pyxides were often tall with a convex body, lug handles and a lid.

Fig. A-86
700–675 B.C.
Height 23 cm.

E. Straight-sided Pyxis

Late 8th century Corinthian pyxides tended to be low with straight sides, no handles, but with a lid.

Fig. A-87
Late 8th century B.C.
Height 11 cm.

F. 'Type I': Tripod Pyxis

Pyxides with a bowl-shaped body and three broad feet were common in Attic pottery in the late 6th century B.C., and then disappeared from production.

Fig. A-88
600–575 B.C.
Height 17½ cm.

G. 'Type II': Low Concave-sided Pyxis

Low pyxides with concave sides, domed lids and low feet were typical Attic and Corinthian forms in the late 5th and throughout the 4th centuries B.C.

Fig. A-89
Late 5th century B.C.
Height 7½ cm.

H. 'Type III': High Concave-sided Pyxis

High concave-sided pyxides with covers having a handle are found in Corinthian pottery from the late 7th century onwards, and in Attic pottery of the 5th century and later.

Fig. A-90
7th century (Corinthian)
Height 10 cm.

Fig. A-91
5th century (Attic)
Height 17 cm.

I. 'Type IV': Normal or Cylindrical Pyxis

The 'normal' pyxis of the 4th century B.C. was a simple round box with straight sides and a flat lid (which had no handle).

Fig. A-92
4th century B.C.
Height 8·5 cm.

10 Cups

Definition: Cup: a deep or a shallow vessel, with or without handles.

Use: For drinking wine.

Size: Varied widely:
Height: from 6 to 25 cm. or 2·5 to 10 inches
Diameter: from 11 to 52 cm. or 4·25 to 20·5 inches
(Normal: 25 to 30 cm.)

Types:
A. Skyphos (or Kotyle) — Proto-Geometric to Hellenistic.

B. Kantharos — Geometric to Hellenistic.

C. Kyathos (or Tea Cup) — Proto-Geometric to first half of 5th century B.C.

D. Other Deep Cups
Megarian and Hemispheric Bowls — 4th to 3rd centuries B.C.
Mastos, Rhyton, etc.

E. Kylix (or Cylix)
Low-based — Geometric to Hellenistic.
Pedestal and Stemmed
Comast Cup — 585–535 B.C.
Siana Cup — 575–550 B.C.
Type I or Lip Cup — 565–535 B.C.
Band Cup — 550–520 B.C.
Type C Cup — 490–460 B.C.
Classical Cup — 480–323 B.C.
Type II or Type A Cup — 550–500 B.C.
Type III or Type B Cup — 520–450 B.C.
Other Shallow Cups

F. Phiale

Note: The so-called 'Little Master' cups include both lip and band cups, and are named from the style of painting rather than from their shape.

SILHOUETTES OF MAIN TYPES

Scale: 1 cm. = 10 cm.

A. Skyphos or Kotyle

The deep cup with two horizontal handles, no stem and a low or pedestal base is called a skyphos or kotyle by archaeologists. Evidence from ancient writings indicates that the word kotyle was the generic name for all cups and that the correct name for this particular type is skyphos. The name kotyle, however, is commonly used. This type of cup was common from the Proto-Geometric period up to the Hellenistic period. Variations appeared for briefer periods.

1. *Proto-Geometric Skyphos*

Fig. A-93
Height 15 cm.

2. *Geometric Skyphos*

Fig. A-94
Height 6·7 cm.

3. *Corinthian Skyphoi*

Corinthian skyphoi were common from the Late Geometric period to the Hellenistic period. Notable for their remarkably thin walls, they are among the finest of Corinthian pottery.

Fig. A-95
Height 9 cm.

Fig. A-96
Height 10·5 cm.

4. *Attic Skyphoi*

   a. Type I: Handles curve upward and are placed below the rim of the cup.

Fig. A-97
c. 500 B.C.
Height 16 cm.

   b. Type II: Level or almost level handles placed level with the rim of the cup, torus foot.

Fig. A-98
c. 460 B.C.
Height 16 cm.

Fig. A-99
Special variety with one handle set horizontally and the other vertically
c. 480 B.C.
Height 10 cm.

B. Kantharos

Deep cups with two tall, vertical handles are known as kantharoi. The base may be low or pedestal and the cup may be stemmed or unstemmed. Though frequently represented in vase-painting, the form was not common in Attic pottery. Metal was probably the usual material, since the high curving handles are not well adapted to ceramics.

1. *Geometric Kantharos*

Fig. A-100
Attic Geometric kantharos
725–700 B.C.
Height including handles 17 cm.

2. *Attic Kantharoi*

Fig. A-101
High-stemmed Attic kantharos
c. 490–480 B.C.
Height including handles 24 cm.

Fig. A-102
Short-stemmed Attic kantharos
c. 490–480 B.C.
Height including handles 18 cm.

Fig. A-103
Low-handled, low-footed
Attic kantharos
c. 450 B.C.
Height 11 cm.

3. *Etruscan Kantharos*

Fig. A-104
Etruscan Bucchero kantharos
7th to 8th centuries B.C.
Height including handles 23 cm.

C. Kyathos and 'Tea Cup'

1. The kyathos is a ladle in the form of a deep cup with a tall vertical handle. Most of these were probably made of metal. Pottery examples

date chiefly from the late 6th century and first half of the 5th century B.C.

Fig. A-105
Attic kyathos
c. 540–520 B.C.
Height including handles 15 cm.

2. The 'tea cup' is another type of deep cup with one vertical handle which, however, does not project above the rim of the cup. In the Proto-Geometric period it had a high conical foot; later this was eliminated.

Fig. A-106
'Tea cup'
Height 9·2 cm.

D. Other Deep Cups

1. *'Megarian' Bowls* and *'Hemispheric' Bowls:* Deep cups without handles, 4th to 3rd centuries B.C.

Fig. A-107
'Megarian' bowl
3rd century B.C.
Diameter 12 cm.

Fig. A-108
'Hemispheric' bowl
3rd century B.C.
Diameter 13 cm.

2. *Mastos:* A deep cup shaped like a woman's breast.

Fig. A-109
Note: one handle vertical, the other horizontal
c. 530 B.C.
Height 10 cm.

3. *Rhyton:* A deep horn-shaped cup or cup in the form of an animal head. Found throughout Greek painted pottery. When filled, the animal head looked down. When empty, the rim of the cup served as the base of the rhyton. Thus when standing, the design on the cup part was upside-down.*

---

* In this, the rhyton differed from the head cup, which is not illustrated here. The latter, made in the form of a human head, rested on the base of the human neck, while the cup, set on top of the head, looked like a crown, or as though it were being carried, balanced on the head.

Fig. A-110
c. 460 B.C.
Height 25 cm.

4. *Chiot Chalice:* The chalice of Chios was a typical form from the late 7th century to the mid 6th century.

Fig. A-111
Height 14 cm.

5. *Others:*

Fig. A-112
Handle-less deep cup, offset
flaring mouth, no foot
End of 6th or early 5th
century B.C.
Height 9 cm.

Fig. A-113
Mug or jug, one handle and
no foot; may have served
as a measure
End of 6th century B.C.
Height 9 cm.

Scale: 1 cm. = 5 cm.

Fig. A-114
Handle-less cup of the
'kalathos' type
Second half of 6th century B.C.
Height 9 cm.

E. Kylix (or Cylix)

1. *Low-based Kylikes*

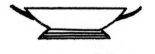

Fig. A-115
Stem-less kylix or bosal
Diameter 27 cm.

Fig. A-116
Corinthian kylix
Late Geometric to
Proto-Corinthian
Diameter 11 cm.

Fig. A-117
East Greek bird bowl
7th and 6th centuries B.C.
Diameter 13 cm.

Fig. A-118
Laconian kylix
c. 6th century B.C.
Diameter 19½ cm.

2. Pedestal and Stemmed Kylikes

a. Attic 'Type I' or Lip Cups: lip and foot offset from bowl.

Fig. A-119
Lip cup of 'Comast' type*
Note low concave mouth, fairly deep bowl, lack of stem, and concave pedestal foot
First quarter of 6th century B.C.
Diameter 21 cm.

Fig. A-120
Lip cup of 'Siana' type*
Note lip and pedestal foot are somewhat higher
Second quarter of 6th century B.C.
Diameter 26·5 cm.

Fig. A-121
Lip cup, 'Little Master' type†
Note relatively tall and sturdy stem, lip and handle zones are reserved
Third quarter of 6th century B.C.
Diameter 32 cm.

Fig. A-122
Lip cup of 'Band Cup' type†
Note tall slim stem, lip painted black, handle zone reserved for decoration
Third quarter of 6th century B.C.
Diameter 26·5 cm.

* See Appendix 1, V, 2a, (1).
† The 'Little Masters' painted both the type of Fig. A–121 and the band cup type of Fig. A–122. Collectively, both types are called 'Little Master' cups from the point of view of decoration, though as shapes they are distinct. See also Appendix 1, V, 2b.

Fig. A-123
Lip cup, 'Type C'*
Note lower stem, very definite
foot, separation of foot from
stem by a fillet, and that stem
and bowl merge in a curve
490–460 B.C.
Diameter 23 cm.

Fig. A-124
Lip cup, Classical period
Note ribbed body with flat
bottom and ridge between body
and stem, and large handles
rising higher than lip
Mid 4th century B.C.
Diameter 17 cm.

b. Attic 'Type II' or 'Type A': Lip forms a continuous curve with
the bowl; foot offset and separated from bowl by a fillet or ridge.†

Fig. A-125
Note quasi-conical foot, ridge
at juncture of foot and bowl
is small
c. 550 B.C.
Diameter 25 cm.

Fig. A-126
Note foot is higher; ridge at
juncture of foot and bowl more
pronounced
c. 550 B.C.
Diameter 20 cm.

Fig. A-127
'Eye cup'
Note bowl is less deep, ridge at
juncture of foot and bowl even
more pronounced
540–530 B.C.
Diameter 32 cm.

Fig. A-128
'Eye cup'
Note shallower bowl, broad
heavy foot, less pronounced
ridge between foot and bowl –
form used by potter Nikosthenes
525–500 B.C.
Diameter 37 cm.

* For 'Type A' and 'Type B' see Figs. A-125–129 and A-130–132.
† See Appendix 1, V, 2b.

Fig. A-129
'Eye cup'
Note foot is lower and more slender
c. 520 B.C.
Diameter 30·5 cm.

c. Attic 'Type III' or 'Type B': Lip, bowl and stem form one continuous curve, except that there is a slight step above the disc of the foot to mark the bottom of the stem. This type superseded Type II or Type A as the favourite shape in about 520 B.C.

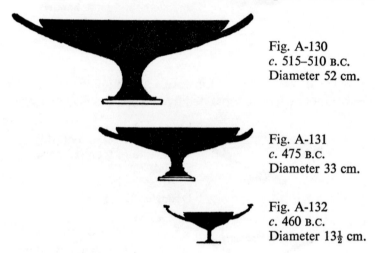

Fig. A-130
c. 515–510 B.C.
Diameter 52 cm.

Fig. A-131
c. 475 B.C.
Diameter 33 cm.

Fig. A-132
c. 460 B.C.
Diameter 13½ cm.

d. Other shallow cups with handles:

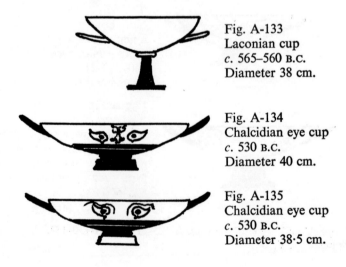

Fig. A-133
Laconian cup
c. 565–560 B.C.
Diameter 38 cm.

Fig. A-134
Chalcidian eye cup
c. 530 B.C.
Diameter 40 cm.

Fig. A-135
Chalcidian eye cup
c. 530 B.C.
Diameter 38·5 cm.

F. Phiale

A low, stemless, shallow cup without handles, for drinking and pouring libations; often had a central boss.

Scales: 1 cm. = 5 cm.   1 cm. = 10 cm.

Fig. A-136
Ribbed to imitate
metal work
c. 460 B.C.
Diameter 16½ cm.

11 Plates and Dishes

A. Plate or Pinax

A flat or flattish disc, with a rim and often a low foot, varying in size from 15 inches (38 cm.) down to fairly small. Plates vary with regard to lip which may be horizontal or oblique, and curl in or curl out; foot may vary from low foot or mere rim to nothing at all. Pottery pinakes were common only in the 6th century B.C. They were probably of wood originally, and later of metal.

1. *Fish Plate:* So-called from fish decorations; downturned rim, disc slopes in to a centre hollow, ring foot, diameter 8–10 inches (20–25 cm.).

B. Dish

Name given to almost any sizeable shallow bowl.

1. *'Wild Goat' Style: c.* 600 B.C., large with simple rim and high stem, others with flat, wide rim, high stem or ring foot.

2. *Attic and Boeotian:* Mid 5th century, large shallow basin with narrow ring foot, flat vertical slip and two recurving handles.
   Scale: 1 cm. = 10 cm.

Fig. A-137
Chiot dish
7th century B.C.
Diameter 38 cm.

C. Lekanis

A flat bowl with a cover, two handles set horizontally and a rim to receive the lid, mid 6th century to the 3rd century B.C.
Scale: 1 cm. = 10 cm.

Fig. A-138
Attic lekanis
c. 420 B.C.
Height 19 cm.

Fig. A-139
South Italian lekanis
3rd century B.C.

D. Other Covered Bowls

Other covered bowls varied in shape. Some had one handle, others had none.

Scale: 1 cm. = 10 cm.

Fig. A-140
One-handled covered bowl
Second half of
5th century B.C.
Height 9 cm.

Fig. A-141
Handle-less covered bowl
Second half of
5th century B.C.
Height 9½ cm.

12 Miscellaneous Shapes

A. Plemochoe

The plemochoe was a vase with a turned-in rim, a high foot and a lid. It was used for carrying perfumes for use in bathing and in religious ceremonies.

Scales: 1 cm. = 5 cm.   1 cm. = 10 cm.

Fig. A-142
End of 6th century B.C.
Height 17 cm.

B. Psykter

The psykter was a wine cooler.

1. *Normal Psykter:* The normal form was a single-walled, high-stemmed bowl with a narrow mouth and broad body drawn in towards the base. It was set in a krater full of cold water or snow. This type appeared in Attic pottery in the late 6th century B.C. and lasted for about fifty years.
Scale: 1 cm. = 10 cm.

Fig. A-143
Normal psykter
c. 480–470 B.C.
Height 28½ cm.

2. *Double-walled Psykter:* A type of double-walled amphora with a spout appeared in Attic pottery only in the 6th century B.C.
Scale: 1 cm. = 10 cm.

Fig. A-144
Double-walled psykter
c. 550–540 B.C.
Height 32 cm.

C. Lebes, Lebes Gamikos

The lebetes were deep bowls with round bottoms made to be set on a stand. Sometimes they had a foot or feet. They were apparently given as prizes in games and were used for mixing wine. The name *dinos* also is frequently applied to this shape but this usage does not appear to be borne out in the ancient writings. The lebes gamikos was a special wedding bowl.

Scale: 1 cm. — 10 cm.

Fig. A-145
Attic lebes gamikos
Mid 4th century B.C.
Height 46 cm.

Fig. A-146
Attic lebes gamikos with double handles and simple stand
590–440 B.C.
Height 66 cm.

Fig. A-147
Lebes or so-called 'dinos'
without handles on tall
stand.
Frequent in 'Wild Goat'
Style of East Greek pottery
and in Early Attic
Black Figure pottery
c. 590 B.C.
Height 93 cm.

Appendix 3
CLAYS AND SLIPS

Clays and Slips

The lists below summarize information relative to clays and slips. Caution is necessary as both clays and slips varied widely. No list, therefore, can be in any sense absolute.

Period	Type	Clay	Slip
Mycenaean		Fine, light brown	Light cream and buff
Proto-Geometric		Poorer texture, light brown	None
Geometric		Fine, light brown, a little darker than Proto-Geometric	Slips reappeared on Laconian, Cycladic and Chiot pottery
Archaic			
	Attic	Fine, orange-red: free from mica	Yellowish on Proto-Attic; buff 610–580 B.C.; and orange-red 580–470 B.C. Also white – became white ground of lekythos
	Corinthian	Fine, smooth, pale, whitish clay, fired to yellowish or pinkish prior to 625 B.C., afterwards to greenish	Orange (coloured with red ochre) after 575 B.C.
	Laconian	Coarse to fine, pink	Cream
	Cretan	Medium fine, brownish	Pale
	Cycladic	Coarse, brownish to red	Yellowish to creamy
	East Greek	Coarse, buff to pink	White (Chiot), others cream to yellow
	Boeotian	Coarser than Attic and paler	At first, creamy, later white, then similar to Attic

Period	Type	Clay	Slip
Archaic (*contd.*)	Euboean	Usually fine, sometimes chalky, similar to Attic –pale brown	None
	Italo-Corinthian	Coarse to fine, light cream to dull brown and slightly muddy, fired to pink	Creamy
	Bucchero	Fine, reduced to grey	Slip reduced to grey
	Etruscan	Not well refined, muddy dirty yellow to pink	Yellowish or reddish
	Chalcidian	Fine, yellow-orange to reddish-brown	Orange-red
	Caeretan	Light yellow brown, warm brown, orange-red	Light to orange
Classical– Hellenistic and Roman			
	Attic	During the 4th century, Attic clay became yellower. In the Hellenistic period, it became less regularly fine and less deep in colour, and tended to be browner	Lighter than on Red Figure ware
	Boeotian	Paler than Attic	
	Corinthian	Yellowish	Orange slip and sometimes a red wash
	Campanian	Light brown	Reddish coating
	West Slope	Less fine than Red Figure Attic	None
	Gnathian	Very varied	None

Period	Type	Clay	Slip
Classical–Hellenistic and Roman (*contd.*)	Lagynos	Fairly fine, micaceous, light brown to reddish	Hard white slip
	Hadra Ware	Light brown to reddish	Yellowish or chalky white
	Canosa Ware	Fairly fine, light brown	White
	Centuripae Ware	Coarse, red to brown	Chalky white
	Pergamene	Fine, yellowish, fired to red or yellow	None
	Arretine	Fired to vivid red	None
	Roman	Coarse to fine, pink	None

Colour Chart

COLOUR CHART

DESIGN COLOURS	DARK				LIGHT						Orange
	Matt Black	Shiny Black	Black to Brown	Reddish-brown	Pale Clay Colour	White Slip	Creamy Slip	Yellowish Slip	Buff to Creamy Buff	Pale Green Clay	
1 Black (shiny)						White-ground Attic Black Figure					
2 Black (shiny) *details:* purple and white*											Attic Black Figure
3 Black *details:* purple, brown, and yellow*									Proto-Corinthian		
4 Black *details:* yellow, white, etc.*									Corinthian Animal Style		Late Corinthian Animal Style (orange slip)
5 Black and Purple* *details:* dull yellow and dull white*								Proto-Attic			
6 Black and Purple* *details:* yellow-brown and bluish-green*								Late Proto-Attic			
7 Black *details:* purple and white*					Laconian I and II						
8 Black (matt–dull)					Proto-Geometric				Middle Helladic		
9 Black to Dark Brown (strong sheen)					Late Geometric						
10 Black to Dark Brown (some sheen)				Mature Geometric							
11 Black to Dark Brown *details:* white				Early Geometric							
12 Black to Brown				Cycladic: Wheel Group			Cycladic: 'AD Group' Cycladic: Heraldic Cycladic: Protome	Cycladic: Theran Cycladic: Linear Is.			
13 Black to Deep Sepia *details:* purple					Laconian III and IV		Laconian III and IV				
14 Dark Brown (matt) *details:* dull purple and white*						East Greek: 'Wild Goat' Style B (streaky slip)	East Greek: 'Wild Goat' Style A				
15 Dark Olive Brown to Golden Brown						Chiot (hard slip)					
16 Light Brown to Purple								Cycladic: Melian			
17 Orange-red *details:* purple		Early and Mature Attic Red Figure									
18 Orange-red *details:* yellow, brownish-yellow, white, red, and gold†		Late Attic Red Figure									
19 Light			Proto-Geometric								
20 Red and White*	Middle Minoan	Middle Minoan									
21 White, Yellow, Purple and Gold†	Hellenistic										
22 Glossy Orange, Orange-red, Red, Brown, and Black (any one of these)									Late Minoan Late Helladic		
23 Pink, Red, Blue, Yellow-brown, Brown, and Black†						Hellenistic		Hellenistic			
24 Matt Black, Red, Purple, Brownish-red, Yellow, Rose, Sky-blue, and Light Purple†						White-ground Attic Red Figure					
25 White, Yellow, Purple, and Gold†	Hellenistic										

* Together
† Usually several colours in combination

Select Bibliography

Arias, P. E., and Hirmer, M.
  A History of Greek Vase Painting, Thames and Hudson, London, 1962
Beazley, J. D.
  Attic Black-Figure Vase-Painters, Clarendon Press, Oxford, 1956
  Attic Red-figured Vases in American Museums, Harvard University
    Press, Cambridge, Mass., 1918
  Attic White Lekythoi, Oxford University Press, London, 1938
  Potter and Painter in Ancient Athens, Geoffrey Cumberlege, London,
    1944
  Attic Red-Figure Vase-Painters, Clarendon Press, Oxford, 1942
  The Development of Attic Black-Figure, University of California
    Press, Berkeley, and Cambridge University Press, London, 1951
Beazley, J. D., and Ashmole, B.
  Greek Sculpture and Painting to the End of the Hellenistic Period,
    University Press, Cambridge, 1932
Buschor, E.
  Greek Vase Painting, trans. G. C. Richards, Chatto and Windus,
    London, 1921 (original German ed., Munich, 1913)
Cook, R. M.
  Greek Painted Pottery, Methuen, London, 1960
Desborough, V. R.
  Protogeometric Pottery, Clarendon Press, Oxford, 1952
Farnsworth, Marie, and Wisely, Harriet
  'Fifth Century Intentional Red Glaze', *Americal Journal of Archeo-
    logy*, Archeological Institute of America, Princeton, N.J., vol. 62,
    no. 2, 1958
Herford, M. A. B.
  A Handbook of Greek Vase Painting, Manchester University, 1919
Hirmer, M., *see* Arias, P. E., and Hirmer, M.
Hoppin, J. C.
  A Handbook of Attic Red-figured Vases, Harvard University Press,
    Cambridge, Mass., 1919, 2 vols.
  A Handbook of Greek Black-figured Vases, Paris, 1924
Lane, A.
  Greek Pottery, Faber and Faber, London, 1948 (new ed., 1963)
Laurie, A. P.
  Greek and Roman Methods of Painting, University Press, Cambridge,
    1910
Noble, J. V.
  'The Techniques of Attic Vase-Painting', *American Journal of*

Archeology, Archeological Institute of America, Princeton, N.J., vol. 64, no. 4, 1960

Payne, H. G. G.
  Necrocorinthia: A Study of Corinthian Art in the Archaic Period, Clarendon Press, Oxford, 1931

Pfuhl, E.
  Masterpieces of Greek Drawing and Painting, trans. J. D. Beazley, Chatto and Windus, London, 1926 (new ed., 1955)

Pottier, F. P. E.
  Douris and the Painters of Greek Vases, trans. Bettina Kahnweiler, John Murray, London, 1909, and Dutton, New York, 1909 (original French ed., 1902)

Richter, G. M. A.
  Attic Red-figured Vases, Metropolitan Museum of Art, New York, 1946 (revised ed., 1958)
  A Handbook of Greek Art, Phaidon Press, London, 1959 (Ch. 11)
  Greek Painting, The Development of Pictorial Representation from the Archaic to Greco-Roman Times, Metropolitan Museum of Art, New York, 1952
  The Craft of Athenian Pottery, Metropolitan Museum of Art, New York, 1923

Richter, G. M. A., and Milne, M. J.
  Shapes and Names of Athenian Vases, Metropolitan Museum of Art, New York, 1935

Robertson, Martin
  Greek Painting, Skira, Geneva, 1959

Seltman, C.
  Attic Vase-Painting, Harvard University Press, Cambridge, Mass., 1933

Swindler, M.
  Ancient Painting, Yale University Press, New Haven, 1929

Walters, H. B.
  History of Ancient Pottery, Greek, Etruscan and Roman, John Murray, London, 1905

Weir, I.
  The Greek Painter's Art, Ginn, Boston, Mass., 1905

White, John
  Perspective in Ancient Drawing and Painting, Society for Promotion of Hellenic Studies, London, 1956

Index of Designs

A

Animals *see also* Lions and Panthers
  angular silhouettes 21, 27–28, 53–61, 109–112
  chequered, hatched, dotted or spotted, 71, 72, 74, 117, 124
  dancing and rubbery 71, 72, 73, 117, 118
  fantastic *see* Mythological creatures
  heraldic, formal poses, in pairs, etc. 22, 63, 73, 113, 114, 117, 118, 145
  outline, curved white faces, bodies various, 21, 29, 58, 62–91, 113–117
  protomes 73, 118
  solid, curved, incised 22, 28–30, 63, 66–70, 81, 86–88, 113–115, 121, 125–129, 136–137
  symbolic 53
  upside-down 128
  wiry, boneless 71–73, 117
Aphrodite 139
Arcs and crescents 53, 79, 122
Athena 30, 129

B

Batons 58
Birds
  angular silhouettes 21, 27–28, 57–61, 109–112
  cross-hatched 62, 71, 79
  droop-tailed 68, 70
  fantastic *see* Mythological creatures
  hatched 119
  heraldic, formal poses, in pairs, etc. 21, 63, 114–115
  others 62, 63, 65, 67, 71, 74, 76, 78–80, 84, 113–117, 119–122, 132, 134–136
  outline, curved, white-faced, bodies various 63, 80–81, 113, 124–125
  solid, curved, incised 81–82, 125–129
  symbolic 53
  upside-down 128, 132, 135
Blobs 70, 71, 116, 118, 121, 127
Brackets 41

C

Cables 29, 47, 63, 65, 68, 69, 71, 74, 76, 77, 81, 83–85, 110, 113, 117–122, 125
Chariots 58, 81, 85, 122, 126, 134, 136
Chequers and/or chessboard design, general 47

bands, panels, etc., chequered 27, 53, 55, 57, 58, 60, 68, 71, 81, 97, 110, 112, 115, 126, 144
Chevrons 48, 58, 60, 68, 71, 109, 112, 118
Circles
  concentric, compass-drawn 27, 48, 53, 54, 57, 110, 111, 112
  concentric, free-hand 48, 53, 74, 76, 77, 79, 110, 111, 117
  concentric, free-hand, heavy 48, 66, 117
  concentric, free-hand, dotted or ringed by dots 48, 71, 72, 74, 76–78, 111, 116, 117
  linked or tied 71, 72, 111, 116
Crescents *see* Arcs
Cross-hatched design, general 47, 54
Crosses 63, 120, 122

D

Dionysiac scenes 29, 92, 139, 141
Dolphins 97, 127, 144, 145
Dotted design, general 47
  misc. dots 63, 64, 115, 118, 122
  spiked dots 118
Double axe *see* Triangles, opposed

E

Eyes as decoration 48, 118, 119, 128, 189, 190

F

Fans 134
Festoons 30, 93, 97, 142, 144, 145
Fish and shellfish 52
Flora and fauna, introduction of, 21, 62
Floral designs *see* specific items (e.g. Garlands, Ivy, Leaves, Lotus, Palmettes, Pomegranates, Rosettes, Vines, Volutes, Wreaths, etc.)
  symbolic, stylized, general 21, 52, 53, 62–64, 73, 79, 113ff
Funeral scenes 58, 93, 112, 141

G

Garlands 92, 97, 139, 145
Geometric designs
  general 21, 53, 57–61, 109–112
  unhatched 53–56, 109–112

General Index

PLATE I. HELLADIC

P.1 (*above*) Two-handled bowl of matt painted ware, dark on light, Middle Helladic: 1900–1580 B.C. Height 7·2 cm. Width (overall) 11·5 cm.

P.2 (*right*) Spouted pitcher with spiral decorations, Late Helladic–Mycenaean: 14th century B.C. Height 28 cm. Width 22·7 cm.

P.3 (*below left*) Jug with cut-away mouth and cuttle-fish design, Late Helladic–Mycenaean: 1580–1100 B.C. Height 27 cm. Width (overall) 24 cm.

P.4 (*below right*) Three-handled amphora with geometric and marine decorations, Late Helladic–Mycenaean: 1580–1100 B.C. Height 48 cm. Width 24 cm.

PLATE II. PROTO-GEOMETRIC

P.5 Amphora with typical concentric semi-circles, wavy lines and broad contrasts of dark and light emphasizing the shoulder and the field between the handles: 10th century B.C. Height 34 cm. Width 27·5 cm.

P.6 (*right*) Hydria with concentric semi-circles and opposed triangles: 10th century B.C. Height 19·5 cm. Width 11·5 cm. *Note the light background (cf. the previous illustration) typical of larger pots of the period.*

P.7 Lekythos, height 20·5 cm. width 13 cm.; goblet, height 14 cm. width 19 cm.; cup with conical foot, height 7 cm.; and oinochoe, height 28 cm. width 17 cm. 10th century B.C. *Note that these smaller pots have dark backgrounds while the larger ones shown in P.5 and P.6 have light backgrounds.*

PLATE III. GEOMETRIC

P.8 Cup with bird design: second half of 8th century B.C. Height 9 cm. Width (overall) 14·5 cm.

P.9 Pyxis with horses as handles on lid: last quarter of 8th century B.C. Height (overall) 19·5 cm. Width 27·5 cm.

P.10 Oinochoe (with tubes) with triangular, bird-headed warriors and spiky horses: end of 8th century B.C. Height 23·5 cm. Width 16·5 cm.

P.11 Jug and lid: end of 8th century B.C. Height 24·5 cm. Width (overall) 15·5 cm.

PLATE IV. ARCHAIC: PROTO-CORINTHIAN

P.12 (*top left*) Oinochoe with hare: 725–625 B.C. *Note the use of parallel lines.* Height 16·5 cm. Width 13 cm.

P.13 (*above*) Aryballos with coursing hound: 7th century B.C. *Note the use of parallel lines.* Height 7·5 cm. Width 4·5 cm.

P.14 (*left*) Aryballos with warriors in the Human Style of Corinth: 625–550 B.C. Height 5 cm. Width 3·3 cm.

P.15 (*below*) Skyphos of typical simplicity, with parallel lines and wavy lines. Measurements are not available.

PLATE V. ARCHAIC: CORINTHIAN

P.16 Animal Style: skyphos with elongated panther typical of the transitional period from the Late Proto-Corinthian to the Early Animal Style: 640–625 B.C. Height 14·5 cm. Width 18·5 cm.

P.17 (*right*) Animal Style: pyxis with fantastic winged animals and incised blob rosettes, typical of the Early Ripe Animal Style: 625–600 B.C. Height (overall) 10·3 cm.

P.18 Animal Style: flat-bottomed oinochoe with incised panther, deer and sphinx, typical of the Animal Style: 625–550 B.C. Height (overall) 23·5 cm. Width 20 cm.

P.19 Animal Style: aryballos with incised bird and incised blob rosettes typical of the Animal Style: *c.* 580 B.C. Height 11·5cm. Width 8 cm.

PLATE VI. ARCHAIC: LACONIAN

P.20 Kylix in the Laconian Black Figure Style: early 6th century B.C. *Note the pomegranate net on the lip and the linked pomegranates on the handle zone.* Height 12·7 cm. Width 18·8 cm.

P.21 Interior of same kylix with sphinx and elaborate border.

P.22 Kylix with typical design: *c.* 550 B.C. Height 12·7 cm. Width (overall) 26·4 cm.

P.23 Interior of preceding kylix.

PLATE VII. ARCHAIC: CYCLADIC

P.24 Pot typical of the Theran sub-Geometric type: 700–675 B.C. Measurements not available.

P.25 Oinochoe typical of the 'Linear Island Group': 700–650 B.C. Height 40 cm.

P.26 Amphora typical of the 'AD Group': 700–650 B.C. Height 49 cm. Width 31 cm.

P.27 Amphora typical of the 'Heraldic Group': 700–650 B.C. Height 48·5 cm. Width 24 cm.

P.28 Amphora typical of the 'Protome Group': c. 650 B.C. Height 32·5 cm. Width 23 cm.

PLATE VIII. ARCHAIC: EAST GREEK

P.29 (*top left*) Rhodian oinochoe of the 'Wild Goat' Style: 700–650 B.C. Height (overall) 35·6 cm.

P.30 (*top right*) Rhodian oinochoe of the 'Wild Goat' Style: 700–650 B.C. Height (overall) 35·9 cm.

P.31 (*lower left*) Rhodian oinochoe of the 'Wild Goat' Style: 650–500 B.C. Height 31 cm.

P.32 (*lower right*) East Greek Fikellura oinochoe with hounds coursing a hare, and crescents typical of Fikellura pottery: 575-500 B.C. Height 27·5 cm.

PLATE IX. ARCHAIC: PROTO-ATTIC

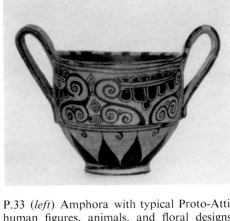

P.33 (*left*) Amphora with typical Proto-Attic human figures, animals, and floral designs: 675–650 B.C. Height 108·5 cm.

P.34 (*above*) Kantharos with typical spirals and other Proto-Attic floral designs: 7th century B.C. Height 6·5 cm. Width 10 cm.

P.35 (*lower left*) Amphora with procession of two-horse chariots; mourning women (on neck); and lions (on shoulder): *c.* 700 B.C. Height 77·7 cm.

P.36 (*below*) Amphora with typical double spirals and oblique meanders: 7th century B.C. Height 52·5 cm. Width 28·5 cm.

PLATE X. ARCHAIC : ATTIC BLACK FIGURE

P.38 (*above*) Siana cup: 575–550 B.C. Height 14 cm. Width (overall) 35 cm.

P.37 (*left*) Amphora with a sphinx by the Nessos (or Nettos) Painter, Early Black Figure: last quarter of 7th century B.C. Height 45·7 cm. Width 34·5 cm.

P.40 (*above*) Band cup: 550–520 B.C. Height 13 cm. Width 27 cm.

P.39 (*left*) Oinochoe of the Mature Black Figure technique: 570–525 B.C. Height 24 cm. Width 14·5 cm.

PLATE XI. ARCHAIC: ATTIC BLACK FIGURE

P.41 (*above*) Panel amphora with horse and rider, Mature Black Figure: 520 B.C. Height 55·7 cm.

P.42 (*top right*) Lekythos showing the entry of Herakles into Olympus, Late Black Figure: 530–500 B.C. Height 31 cm. Width 7 cm.

P.43 (*below left*) Stamnos with Dionysus, satyr and maenads: 6th century B.C. Height 30 cm.

P.44 (*below right*) Lekythos with warrior and horses in the Black Figure technique with white ground: end of 6th century B.C. Height 21·2 cm.

PLATE XII. ARCHAIC: ATTIC RED FIGURE

P.45 (*above*) Inside of kylix showing a girl at an altar, Early Red Figure: 520–500 B.C. Width (overall) 25 cm.

P.48 (*above*) Amphora with Theseus and Skiron: 490–480 B.C. Height 36·7 cm.

P.46 (*above*) Exterior of Attic Type B kylix showing Achilles and Memnon: 520–500 B.C. Height 7·4 cm. Width (overall) 18 cm.

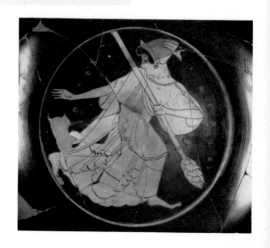

P.47 Inside of cup showing maenad: 520–500 B.C. Width 18·7 cm.

PLATE XIII. CLASSICAL: ATTIC RED FIGURE

P.50 (*above*) Oinochoe showing Ganymede, attributed to the Pan Painter: 470–460 B.C. Height 16·5 cm. Width 11 cm.
P.52 (*below*) Pelike showing King Poly-peithes and two women: 450–440 B.C. Height 55 cm. Width 57·5 cm.

P.49 (*above*) Lekythos with Ripe Archaic Style Athena, attributed to the Painter of the Boston Tithonos: *c.*480 B.C. Height 34·9 cm. Width 11·8 cm.
P.51 (*below*) Calyx krater with battle of Greeks and Romans, attributed to the Painter of the Berlin Hydria: 460–450 B.C. Height 55 cm. Width 57·5 cm.

PLATE XIV. CLASSICAL: ATTIC RED FIGURE

P.54 (*above*) Hydria showing a mistress and her maids in the style of the Kleophon Painter, Classical Attic Red Figure: 435–420 B.C. Height 30 cm.

P.56 (*below*) Pelike with Mousaios and his family, and Muses and goddesses, attributed to the Meidias Painter: 420–400 B.C. Height 47·5 cm.

P.53 (*above*) Oinochoe showing a *nike*, Early Classical Red Figure: 480–450 B.C. Height 21·5 cm. Width 18 cm.

P.55 (*below*) Kylix krater showing the three cloaked youths typically found on the back of Late Classical Red Figure vases: 450–425 B.C. or later. Height 25 cm.

PLATE XV. CLASSICAL: ATTIC RED FIGURE (P.57-59)
ARCHAIC — HELLENISTIC (P.60)

P.57 (*above*) Oinochoe (Type III): 425–400
B.C. Height 7·8 cm. Width 6·1 cm. *Note
the degeneration in the drawing.*
P.59 (*below*) Pyxis (Red Figure on White
Ground) showing the Judgment of Paris,
attributed to the Pentheseleia Painter:
465–460 B.C. Height (overall) 14·3 cm.

P.58 (*above*) Lekythos (Red Figure on
White Ground) showing a trainer in the
palaestra: 5th century B.C. Height 25·5 cm.
P.60 (*below*) Skyphos type cup of 'Black
Glazed Ware': third quarter of 5th century
B.C. Height 3·5 cm. Width (of base) 5·7 cm.

PLATE XVI. HELLENISTIC

P.62 West Slope Ware: 323–146 B.C. *Note the degeneration in the painting and the clumsiness of the shape.* Height 21 cm.

P.61 Kantharos painted and moulded in relief: 323–146 B.C. *Note that the painting is mere decoration.* Height 1·69 cm. Width (overall) 12·1 cm.

P.63 (*left*) Pyxis of typical Light Ground Ware: 323–146 B.C. Height 15·5 cm. Width 12·5 cm.
P.64 (*below*) 'Megarian' bowl: 323–146 B.C. Height 7·5 cm. Width 13·4 cm.